'Forgive an old preacher's use [...] informed, insightful and intere[...] opinions but provides an inforn[...] underpinned by the careful use[...] recent research. It is insightful, legitimately ar[...] many features in Moses' life, several of which are personally quite challenging, which have relevance for our own lives as leaders. It trips along at a good pace with something fresh always ready to maintain interest in the next page. In the crowded shelves of books on Christian leadership this deserves a place. Even better, it deserves to be taken down from the shelf and eagerly read.'

Rev Dr Derek Tidball, former Principal of the London School of Theology

'In this gem of a book, Alan Wilson combines the fruit of many years of reflection on the practice of leadership, both his own and that of others, with profound insights into the wisdom Scripture offers around the exercise of godly leadership. With its emphasis on the personal formation of the leader and on some of the core habits and practices that lead to both faithfulness and effectiveness, this is a resource whose careful study will be of equal benefit to seasoned leaders, those in the early stages of a leadership journey and those preparing for leadership.'

Rev Canon Ian Parkinson, author of Understanding Christian Leadership

'The story of Moses is a rich store of wisdom for leaders and those aspiring to leadership. Alan Wilson has unearthed some gold nuggets that will inform and inspire.'
Ian Coffey, Acting Principal, Moorlands College

'We loved Alan Wilson's book. The life of Moses is covered in depth with insight and accuracy. Alan captures the heart of the story with empathy (he's been there) and with practical steps

and application which will help any Christian enhance their walk with Christ. The chapters on wilderness and God's love for a leader are exceptional. I wish we had read this book forty years ago – it would have saved us from a few blind alleys! Take your leadership through the book, preach through it, recommend it and you and your church will be incredibly blessed.'
Paul and Priscilla Reid, CFC Belfast

'With a clear and accessible style, Alan Wilson shows us from the life of Moses something of the demands, frustrations and rewards of effective leadership of the people of God. By faithful exegesis and application of the text of Scripture, he explores how God can take the inadequate and failed person to do extraordinary things as a leader in their church. To lead like this there are certain things we need to know, which we discover in the life of Moses. This book therefore should be a primary resource for leaders and potential leaders in today's church.'
Dr Trevor Morrow, Minister Emeritus, Lucan Presbyterian Church

'As a leader in my thirties with still so much to learn myself, I am delighted that Alan has put pen to paper to bring us this comprehensive view of leadership. I have valued the teaching and advice of the author first-hand and the words you are about to read are peppered with the same wisdom, humility and passion as he brings in person. With a comprehensive journey through the life and leadership of Moses, Alan's writings are both deeply biblical yet intensely practical, and the personal insights from his own ministry alongside the lessons he has drawn from fellow leaders and authors make for a rich resource. The book will remind you of your primary identity, reassure you in the midst of personal crisis, reorient your view of leadership and reveal a mix of fresh insights and ancient truth that will enrich your leadership.'
Rick Hill, Presbyterian Church in Ireland; author of Deep Roots of Resilient Disciples

'Few things are more important than wise leadership in every area of life. Thank you, Alan, for a great book identifying vitally crucial leadership lessons. Skilfully and thoughtfully you highlight, from the life of Moses, some priority and very timely issues for all in leadership. Your book is biblical, practical and totally life related. Leaders are always wearing L-plates, and this book will not disappoint all who are eager to learn more about being wise leaders!'
Bishop Ken (Fanta) Clarke, author of Going for Growth

'In *The Crucible of Leadership: Learning from the Story of Moses*, Alan Wilson looks closely at the highs and lows of Moses' life and ministry to draw out important lessons for Christians in leadership. This engaging book, illuminated with biblical insights and personal illustrations, draws out vital principles for wise leaders. From foundations and formation to finishing well, *The Crucible of Leadership* focuses on character rather than charisma, on integrity and identity rather than skills or techniques. Enriched as it is from the author's own wide and long experience of leadership, the tone is gentle and humble, pointing always to the central place of a relationship with God at the heart of the leadership journey. Highly recommended!'
Ruth Garvey-Williams, Editor of VOX *magazine*

'This is a book that draws you in and feeds your soul. Each chapter is packed with wisdom and insight, with Alan's pastor's heart setting a gracious tone that is evident throughout. In this book we have a perceptive collection of thoughts on leadership that speak with timely accuracy to our leadership practice, as well as prophetic revelation to always keep our eyes and ears on God Himself.'
Dr Helen Warnock, Former Principal of Belfast Bible College

'As the title of this book wisely suggests, development of God-centred leadership is difficult and a lifelong process, yet it is so deeply fulfilling and so desperately needed in whatever sphere of influence God has led you into. For me, the crux of this intentional development is an ongoing grasp of Alan's chapter 5 heading: 'Wise leaders know that God loves them'. It seems such a simple thought, yet how easily is it forgotten! I'm thankful for that crucial reminder, and for everything else that ripples out from such a foundational truth.'

Edwin Backler, Company Chairman and Leadership Coach

'At a time when many feel discouraged and disorientated, this book carries a timely message to strengthen, challenge and reorientate those called to lead. From the depths of Alan's personal experience, wide research and insightful biblical reflection, I believe this book will both stimulate your thinking and stir your spirit.'

Rev Simon Genoe, New Wine Ireland

'In a well-populated market of books on leadership, Alan Wilson's treatment of the theme sets itself apart by being sensitive to the text of Scripture and attentive to the real-time rigours of leadership. Microscopic in its assessment of Moses' leadership, empathetic in its approach to the reader and synthetic in its combination of precept and narrative, this text occupies a vital space among literature dealing with the formation and maturation of the leader's heart and life.'

Pastor Andrew Roycroft, Portadown Baptist Church

'I am drawn to leadership books that reinforce the truth that successful leadership is about more than how many people follow you or what you have accomplished, but rather about who you are becoming. Christian leaders need to always remember that they are being called and crafted by God, are in an ongoing process of spiritual growth, and are dependent on the gifts of others. Leadership doesn't belong to us but to the One who has called us and loves us. Employing the story of

Moses, *The Crucible of Leadership* is a powerful, personal, and practical reminder of all of these things. There is no leader who wouldn't benefit from this book.'
Paul David Tripp, Author of Lead: 12 Gospel Principles for Leadership in the Church *and* New Morning mercies: a Daily Gospel Devotional

'The subtitle of this most helpful book is *Learning from the story of Moses*. But in just ten, punchy chapters, we are introduced to a wide range of biblical characters and truth. It is a goldmine of pithy quotations, great illustrations, and insightful and wise practical and pastoral applications. Timely, biblical, well-written and researched, it certainly has done me a power of good, and I believe it will do the same for any reader. Highly recommended!'
Dr Steve Brady, First Baptist Church of Grand Cayman; President, Moorlands College

THE CRUCIBLE OF LEADERSHIP

Learning from the Story of Moses

Alan Wilson

instant apostle

First published in Great Britain in 2022

Instant Apostle
104 The Drive
Rickmansworth
Herts
WD3 4DU

British Library Cataloguing-in-Publication Data

A catalogue record for this book is available from the British Library.

This book and all other Instant Apostle books are available from Instant Apostle:

Website: www.instantapostle.com

Email: info@instantapostle.com

ISBN 978-1-912726-57-8

Printed in Great Britain.

Acknowledgements

This book is offered with thanks to all those leaders who have shared their stories with me, to friends who read early drafts, to the team at Instant Apostle for giving the enterprise wings (and proper punctuation), to Pauline, who has unselfishly supported me in this project and in so much more besides, and to the Lord, for His patience.

It is offered to its readers in the hope that it will help leaders to lead well.

Contents

Introduction:
(Yet) Another Book on Leadership

Of making many books there is no end, and much study
wearies the body.
(Ecclesiastes 12:12)

In writing this book I am well aware that I am adding to what is already an extensive and rapidly growing pile on the subject of leadership. Indeed, if I may paraphrase Ecclesiastes, 'of making many books on leadership, there is no end'.

Recent decades have seen an exponential increase in the number of books on the subject, and when you add in the conferences, seminars and podcasts, there is no shortage of material, whether inside or outside the Church. Few people would dispute that leadership – whatever exactly it is – matters.

But what exactly is it? Leadership scholar Warren Bennis once wrote that to some degree 'leadership is like beauty: it's hard to define, but you know it when you see it'.[1] Not that the difficulty has prevented people from trying to define it: there are hundreds of definitions out there. I'm not going to list them or attempt to add something novel to them: suffice to say that something along the lines of 'influencing people in the direction of a mutually beneficial goal' won't go far wrong.

Beyond general questions of definition, Christians wonder if there is such a thing as Christian leadership, and if there is (and it sounds like there should be), then what should it look like and what would set it apart as particularly Christian?

Perhaps it's an unnecessary quest: if it's true that leadership is leadership, then why not simply take all the highlights from the best of what's out there? After all, no one is on a mission to develop a specifically Christian approach to cardiology or to electrical engineering. A few doses of Jack Welch, the former CEO of General Electric, mixed with pithy lessons from football legend Sir Alex Ferguson, or whatever other leader is currently catching the imagination of the public, all nicely held together with a few gems from emotional intelligence exponent Daniel Goleman should do the trick.

On the other hand, there are quite a few leaders in the Bible, so perhaps we ought to pay some attention to them. But what happens when the Bible – or at least, certain parts of it – is reduced to being a primer on leadership? What if, instead of being read as a record of God's faithfulness to His people and His plan, the story of Nehemiah becomes 'Leadership 101'? I've no doubt that there are many

[1] Warren Bennis, *On Becoming a Leader* (London: Arrow Business Books, 1998), p1.

pertinent and transferable observations to be made about the leadership of Nehemiah, but we need to be wary of turning the Bible into a source book for whatever theory or idea we want to find there, while abandoning any attention to its divine intent.

A further caution comes from author and scholar Arthur Boers, who fears that Christians have bought too quickly into the 'fads' of leadership, without adequately allowing Scripture to critique their ideas.[2] He argues that the basic posture of Scripture towards the concept of human leadership is one of suspicion, and raises the possibility that the problem with human leadership is not simply that there are too many flawed leaders, but that there is something inherently problematic about the whole enterprise. Whether or not this is overstating the case, the Bible certainly has plenty to say about the flaws and failures of human leadership, not to mention its treatment of the hubris and arrogance of human leaders who set themselves against God.

Despite the cautions, here I am, adding to the pile.

Learning from Moses

A few years ago I was invited to speak to a group of pastors who wanted me to share some of the things I had learned about ministry. I've been in and around Christian ministry for several decades, both as a church leader, in Switzerland and in Northern Ireland, and as an observer of leaders and leadership. My work has included an

---

[2] Arthur Boers, *Servants and Fools: A Biblical Theology of Leadership* (Nashville, TN: Abington, 2015).

academic research project that explored the concept of 'crucible' experiences in the development of Christian leaders, and my interest in leaders' stories has continued at a more popular level with a series of interviews under the rubric of *The Leadership Journey Podcast*.[3]

I decided to set my reflections for the group within the framework of Moses' story, and so was born the list of lessons that make up the main part of this book. My aim is to impart not so much a 'how to' that will help you increase your mastery of the technical side of leadership, as a 'what's happening?' that I hope will actually help you become a better leader as you reflect on the personal side of leadership: the best leadership flows from who the leader is rather than merely the skills the leader has mastered.

Not only is Moses one of the most significant theological figures in the Bible, not least as the one through whom the 'law was given' (John 1:17), but he was also one of the great biblical leaders. His leadership has been widely admired and widely reflected on. For example, Ruth Haley Barton writes this about her fascination with Moses:

> I have been drawn to the story of Moses because
> I have found it to be so complete in illustrating
> the different aspects of leadership and so

[3] The podcast is available at www.yourleadershipjourney.net (accessed 7th October, 2021); the academic study can be downloaded from the University of Chester: chesterrep.openrepository.com/handle/10034/620752 (accessed 7th October 2021).

unflinchingly honest about the challenges leaders experience.[4]

I think she's right about the leadership value of his story.

Perhaps you have heard the homely summary of Moses' life that is often attributed to American evangelist D L Moody. Moody is reputed to have said that 'Moses spent forty years thinking he was somebody, forty years learning he was nobody, and forty years discovering what God can do with a nobody'. I'm not sure where I first heard that but it has stuck with me.[5] Our lives may not fall into such evenly distributed chronological sections, but it seems to me that Moses' story (not least as interpreted by Moody) gives us a useful way to think about the progression of a leadership journey.

His formative years were spent in Egypt, where he had been born into a family of Hebrew slaves, but remarkably ended up being raised as a member of the royal family. A failed attempt to lead a liberation movement resulted in his being pitched unceremoniously into the wilderness – forty years spent in the Midianite desert where the peak of his career appears to have been taking care of his father-in-law's sheep – quite a contrast with some of the traditional understandings of his time in Egypt which tell tales of military prowess! Finally, after a remarkable encounter with God on the edge of the desert, his life takes another dramatic turn and he becomes a reluctant leader,

---

[4] Ruth Haley Barton, *Strengthening the Soul of Your Leadership: Seeking God in the Crucible of Ministry* (Downers Grove, IL: IVP, 2008), p18.
[5] I have no original source for the quote, but it can be traced at least as far as Henrietta C Mears, *What the Bible is All About* (Ventura: CA: Gospel Light Publications, 1966), p33.

going on to spend the next forty years navigating the highs and lows of leadership in the desert. Although those forty years ended in disappointment for Moses, they nonetheless gave him the privilege of seeing God's greatness and His strong hand.

Along the way there are influential characters, defining moments, high points and lows and plenty of lessons for today's leaders to observe and assimilate.

I should say that what follows is not intended as a systematic exposition of the Pentateuch, or at least those parts that contain the accounts of Moses' life and leadership. I'm aware of the debates on the subject of their historicity, but they're beyond the scope of this book and I'll leave it to others to sort through them.[6] My goal is to explore the crucible of leadership, and to do so by weaving together various ideas and reflections on leaders and leadership, framing them in the context of the story of Moses as it has come down to us in our Bible.

For leadership is a crucible. Put another way, it's a life-defining journey in which a leader not only shapes an organisation or a historic moment, but one during which the leader too is shaped.

---

[6] For a discussion from an evangelical perspective, see Tremper Longman, *How to Read Exodus* (Downers Grove: IL: IVP Academic, 2009), or T Desmond Alexander, *Exodus*, Apollos Old Testament Commentary (London: Apollos, 2017).

Who's the book for?

While I want the book to be helpful particularly for people in what I would call 'vocational Christian leadership', I hope its appeal will be wider.

For some time now, much of the Church has tended to segregate spiritual leadership from secular leadership, meaning that pastors, bishops, mission leaders and heads of Christian charities are viewed somewhat differently from the Christian head of a bank, or a Christian who happens to be a senior leader in the United Nations. However, it's a mistake to think that God is only interested in the former group or that it's only church ministers and their ilk whose leadership is in any sense spiritual. Although church leadership is far from easy – and I think it will continue to become more complex and challenging in years to come – some of the biggest leadership challenges are those faced by leaders who seek to integrate their faith in potentially hostile spaces outside the Church.

Among the most significant examples of God-centred leadership in the Bible are those that take place in what we might classify as 'secular' environments. Joseph had a remarkable relationship with God and was endowed with exceptional wisdom and insight: while ultimately he was serving God's redemptive purposes, the immediate beneficiaries of his skill were the Egyptians. Similarly, Daniel rose through the ranks of Babylonian bureaucracy as the Lord blessed his devotion and commitment while giving notice that the God of Israel was by no means confined to His temple in Jerusalem.

In the same way, some of us will find that our leadership takes place in settings outside the formal bounds of 'church': how will we relate that sphere to God?

Ideally, then, the book is for anyone who wants to explore the connection between their leadership and their relationship with God. Even if you are not a leader, but you have an interest in better understanding some of the dynamics of leadership, I hope the book will be helpful.

Despite my desire to be wide-ranging in relevance, I suspect that it will be hard to hide my church leadership leaning, since that is the sphere with which I am most familiar.

I should also add that the book is not intended to be exhaustive: why stop at eight lessons (nine, with the epilogue), as if that's all there are, or why this particular set rather than a different one? If you have been involved in spiritual leadership for any length of time, you could probably add quite quickly and easily to my list.

- Chapter One explores the idea that few of us arrive as leaders without the help and influence of other people. Had it not been for the quick thinking and courage of his mother and sister, the outcome of Moses' story would have been quite different.

- In Chapter Two the focus moves to the middle years of Moses' life, spent 'in exile' in the Midianite wilderness. We'll refer to what Robert Clinton and Shelley Trebesch describe as 'isolation',[7] where a

[7] See Robert Clinton, *The Making of a Leader* (Colorado Springs, CO: NavPress, 1988); Shelley Trebesch, *Isolation: A Place of Transformation in the Life of a Leader* (Altadena: CA: Barnabas Publishers, 1997).

leader finds him or herself set aside from their normal sphere of leadership.

- In Chapter Three we look at the remarkable tale of Moses' call, as he desperately tries to find ways of getting out of a task that we suspect he would have jumped at forty years previously.

- Chapter Four explores the idea that ministry is meant to be a shared enterprise. On two occasions we find Moses overwhelmed at the magnitude of his responsibility: once when he is rescued by the wisdom of his father-in-law, and once when God pours out His Spirit on community elders.

- Chapter Five picks up on a theme that emerged from my research and that I have noticed in the telling of several leaders' stories: a personal assurance of the love of God. Aside from the privilege of seeing God's power at work in deliverance and ongoing provision, Moses was blessed to hear God say that He knew him by name and that he had 'found favour' in His sight (Exodus 33:17, ESV).

- Chapter Six explores the challenges of conflict and criticism. Moses knew plenty of them, and contemporary leaders need to accept that they too will face these challenges, and will need to find ways to navigate them.

- In Chapter Seven we explore the issue of character as we consider the second rock-striking episode, a sad failure that saw Moses barred from entering the land of promise. His failure is a reminder that our character remains a work in progress.

- Chapter Eight then reminds us that none of us stays around to lead forever, and explores the story of Moses and Joshua as a way of asking how a new generation of leaders can emerge who will pick up the baton of leadership.

- In the Epilogue we revisit the rock-striking episode and see that spiritual leadership should point to Jesus: the leader should not get in His way.

Welcome to the crucible of leadership.

1
Wise Leaders Know That They Don't Get There By Themselves

By faith Moses' parents hid him for three months after he was born, because they saw he was no ordinary child, and they were not afraid of the king's edict.
(Hebrews 11:23)

None of us gets to choose the time or circumstances of our birth.

In his thought-provoking book *Turas*, which envisages a group of Northern Irish Presbyterians attempting to come to terms with an imagined United Ireland, one of Colin Neill's characters makes this observation:

> I never fail to marvel at how much of a person's character and experience often seems the consequence of a random chance of birth. Think of the Kamikaze pilot flying his plane into American aircraft carriers off the coast of his homeland. Think of the civil rights marchers thronged behind their banners in the Deep

South. Think of the North Koreans who live and then die within such a narrow tunnel of opportunity that oppression is numbed only by their not knowing how oppressed they are. If God in his providence had set all these people, made in his own image, in another time and place, their lives would have been completely different.[8]

Imagine how different your life might have been if you had been born 100 years earlier, and on the other side of the world. What if you had been born to different parents or born into a different race, with a different skin colour?

The shape of so many aspects of our lives is influenced by things that are totally beyond our control and by decisions made by other people.

So it was with Moses. He was not consulted about any of the circumstances into which he would be born. No one asked him to choose the historical era of his birth; no one asked how he felt about being born into a race of slaves at one of the low points in their history. He wasn't asked to indicate his preferred choice of parents.

The Scottish philosopher Thomas Carlyle famously claimed that 'the history of the world is but the biography of great men':[9] he saw these 'great men' as the initiators of whatever was accomplished in the world. The study of leadership has moved far beyond the so-called great man theory, but we can't dismiss all the implications of

[8] Colin Neill, *Turas* (Leicester: Matador, 2011), pxiii. Used with permission.

[9] Thomas Carlyle, *On Heroes, Hero-Worship and the Heroic in History* (New York: Cosimo, 2010), p41.

Carlyle's statement, for we too expect leaders to shape their times.

The other side of that coin is that leaders are also products of their times. Indeed, how many of history's great names might have been consigned to obscurity had it not been for the particular circumstances that formed them, or that called for their unique gifts of leadership?

The birth of Moses

Moses' ancestors had settled in Egypt many generations previously, a legacy of the remarkable influence of Joseph at a time of national crisis. However, the passage of time had brought with it the fading of memory, and eventually a king (possibly Ramses II) 'to whom Joseph meant nothing' (Exodus 1:8) came to power. To him and his people, this burgeoning group of resident foreigners represented something of a problem: they could not be allowed to become so numerous that they might join with hostile external forces in the event of a war, and so escape, something that would doubtless have reduced Pharaoh's labour force.

The narrative in Exodus 1 traces the Egyptians' attempt to resolve their Israelite problem. First came hard labour. Then came a campaign of racially based infanticide where the Hebrew midwives were told to kill newborn Hebrew boys while letting the girls live. The midwives refused to comply, and were rewarded by God with children of their own.

Sadly, their resistance was not the final piece of the story, as responsibility for eliminating newborn Hebrew boys passed to the Egyptians who were to throw the boys into the Nile.

These were desperate times.

No one ever gets to choose the circumstances of their birth but, were it possible, no one would choose to be born into this.

However, at the same time there was another reality. The Israelites were people of promise. God had promised their ancestor, Abraham, that he would become 'a great nation' (Genesis 12:2). He had also foretold the long years during which they would live as aliens and slaves (Genesis 15:13). But that time would pass and their future would be prosperous.

Pivotal to this transformation in their fortunes would be Moses.

There is something about the way Exodus tells the story of his birth that ought to catch our attention:

> Now a man of the tribe of Levi married a Levite woman, and she became pregnant and gave birth to a son.
> (Exodus 2:1-2)

To all intents and purposes it looks as though we are reading the story of this couple's firstborn. But Moses was not their first child. It soon becomes clear that Moses' parents already had a daughter, and we eventually discover that they also had an older son, born three years previously.

Why, then, is the story told in this way?

One theory is that Moses' parents, Amram and Jochebed, had separated after the birth of their older children, rather than run the risk of bringing another son into the circumstances described in Exodus 1. Jewish tradition claims that it was the intervention of Miriam that in some way shamed her father into re-establishing his marriage, and Moses was the fruit of that union.

While that's an intriguing interpretation of the apparent strangeness of the narrative, it may simply be that the writer has compressed the details of the story, omitting the births of Miriam and Aaron, in order to get to the birth of Moses which, in a sense, is the starting point for the story of redemption that will shortly unfold.

Either way, Moses was born into the most precarious of circumstances.

In the church I pastored for seventeen years in Switzerland, new parents had the opportunity to participate in a dedication service for their children. I remember one young father, on the occasion of the birth of his first son, admitting with considerable honesty that he wondered what he had done in introducing a new child to the world.

It's a question any parent might ask. The world, after all, is a dangerous and turbulent place. Of course it has its stunning beauty, and life has the potential to be a wonderful adventure of discovery. But it is a world of political uncertainty, of famine, of climate change, of deep division and much brokenness. How many people's experience of the ragged edges of existence leads them, like Job, to wish they had never been born? Yet, as Jewish author Levi Meier puts it, 'most of us still choose to bring new life into the world'.[10]

There is a sense in which bringing a child into the world is an act of faith. Faith, perhaps, that this child will lead a fruitful life: who knows but that they might discover a new treatment for cancer, or that they might emerge as a significant reforming and life-bringing leader in the Church? Faith that they will bring joy, faith that they will be loved.

If bringing any child into the world may be construed as an act of faith and courage, the dark cloud of Pharaoh's decree underlined the faith and courage of Moses' parents: faith and courage that would soon be further tested.

Three women

Strikingly, the early months of Moses' life were dominated by the parts played by three women.

The first was his mother, Jochebed: it's highly unlikely that she would have regarded her son as anything other than a 'fine child' (Exodus 2:2), but such was the power of maternal affection that she chose to protect him from the fate that had been decreed by Pharaoh.

It's worth noting that the word 'fine' (Hebrew *tov*) is translated 'good' in the telling of the creation story in Genesis. Its first occurrence in Scripture comes in relation to the newly created light – 'God saw that the light was good' (Genesis 1:4). Levi Meier comments that the use of the word points to the birth of Moses as 'the time for

---

[10] Levi Meier, *Moses the Prince, the Prophet* (Woodstock, VT: Jewish Lights, 1999), p12.

another beginning, for new life, for a radiant life force, for positive energy'.[11] Certainly the arrival of this particular baby would prove to be light in the darkness of the Hebrews' experience.

But we need to ask a question: what was it that led this one mother to defy the measures to which others had presumably submitted? Did other mothers not feel the same affection for their sons? Did the instinct to protect Moses involve more than maternal affection?

We should also observe that Hebrews 11 – adding the involvement of Moses' father – tells us that his parents 'saw that the child was beautiful' (v23, ESV) or that 'he was no ordinary child' (NIV), and that Stephen, in his speech to the Jewish Sanhedrin, adds the detail that 'he was beautiful in God's sight' (Acts 7:20, ESV). There was something about this boy that prompted his parents to act in faith, choosing to hide him, refusing to be 'afraid of the king's edict' (Hebrews 11:23).

Whether or not we accept the Jewish explanation of the birth story mentioned earlier, Jochebed and her husband had taken a gamble in conceiving and giving birth to this child. Now that she had given birth to a son, what would she do about the king's edict?

As Hebrews 11 tells it, the answer lies in her (and her husband's) faith. Since their faith was stronger than any fear of the king's edict, they chose to hide their son. In effect they believed that, whatever the king might decree, there was a higher hand. Had Moses' mother not trusted God, but had instead given way to fear, Moses would not

---

[11] Ibid, p17.

have lived and could never have become the leader that Israel needed.

Isn't it humbling to realise that the earliest destiny-shaping decisions in any leader's life may be taken when the leader is totally unaware of them?

But keeping a small child hidden is not easy. All it needed was for one of Pharaoh's loyalists who had believed the anti-Hebrew message emanating from the throne to hear a crying baby in the middle of the night.

After three months of seclusion, it must have become impossible for Jochebed to keep her son hidden. So she sheltered him in a well-prepared papyrus basket and left him among the reeds along the bank of the Nile.

Miriam (Moses' sister is eventually named in Exodus 15) stands nearby to see what will happen, and it is her quick thinking that leads her, in her turn, to contribute to the salvation of her brother. Then, when the third woman appears, the story takes a dramatic twist.

This third woman – in a wonderful touch of delicious irony – is the daughter of Pharaoh, the king who wanted rid of Hebrew boys in the first place. It was when she noticed the basket and discovered the crying Hebrew baby that she was stirred to pity (maybe Moses' mother wasn't the only one to think her son was good-looking). Whatever her personal view of her father's genocidal campaign, a crying baby was to be pitied, not destroyed.

It's here that Miriam proposes a solution. Why not find 'one of the Hebrew women to nurse the baby' (Exodus 2:7)? The result is that, far from being thrown in the Nile, Moses is cared for by his own mother, whose services are recompensed by the daughter of the king who had issued the genocidal decree: rewarded for looking after her own son.

As well as the rich irony of the fact that Pharaoh's own daughter has undermined his scheme – and time will reveal how profoundly undermined it has been, since the man who will be Egypt's nemesis has been allowed to live – we need to notice a further irony in the story.

Pharaoh's solution to his 'Hebrew dilemma' is the elimination of the males: in the providence of God, his plan is subverted by three females. I'm sure there might be some fuel there to kindle the fires of debate on the nature of the ministry of women, but I'll leave that for others, and make these two observations:

- God's plan is advancing while Pharaoh's attention is focused elsewhere (Pharaoh is focused on the obvious – deal with the males);

- God uses people whom the culture finds easy to overlook.

Like the wider culture, the contemporary Church has had its heroes and celebrities. Perhaps we should be careful to distinguish between those terms. Heroes, properly understood, have done something worth admiring; celebrities tend to be famous for being famous (if that's not too cynical). It's probably normal and healthy to have heroes, those whom we respect and aspire to emulate, just as long as we remember their limitations and that they are not deities to be worshipped. Recent years have exposed the flaws in too many of our heroes: a pedestal can be a perilous place. There is truth in the old adage that 'the best of men are but men at the best'.[12]

We fall easily into the trap of assuming that if anything of note is going to happen for the sake of God's kingdom, it will come about as a result of the influence of the big names. It's the speakers with the large platforms and huge gatherings. It's the singers and songwriters with the most recent hit songs. It's the well-known authors or the high-profile leaders that God will use to bring about revival and the transformation of the world. Put like that, it all sounds suspiciously like a Christianised version of Thomas Carlyle's great man theory, mentioned above.

I'm grateful for well-known and gifted writers, singers and speakers who faithfully serve God and bless the Church. And it's not that we should embark on some kind of iconoclastic crusade to chop all such people down to size: we should honour and acknowledge those who serve God well. It's just that we ought to realise that there may be times when our eyes are so intently fixed on the big platforms that we miss the fact that God is working away off stage through the faith and courage of people who may be almost completely unknown beyond their immediate circle of acquaintances. Who can measure what God is doing through the quiet faithfulness of unassuming followers that we have not even noticed?

Arthur Boers puts it like this:

---

[12] It's not known who first said it, but the phrase goes back at least to the seventeenth century, when it was used in reference to a supporter of Oliver Cromwell (see www.bhcarroll.edu/2020/05/the-best-of-men-are-but-men-at-best/) (accessed 26th January 2021).

> While history focuses on victors and the powerful, people at the top and in charge, the Bible pays an astonishing amount of attention to regular, normal folk who are nevertheless the unexpected means of God's dramatic work.[13]

One of the practical pastoral implications of this is that leaders need to honour and encourage those 'regular, normal folk'. Sometimes these are older men and women who have passed the stage where they'd be regarded as movers and shakers. They may well shun publicity and avoid platforms, but they may be the ones through whom the Lord is advancing the work of His kingdom.

And if you are one of those quiet, understated folk, be encouraged. God knows your name. Not only were the Hebrew midwives who defied Pharaoh blessed with children, but their names are recorded in Scripture: the name of the Pharaoh is not.

Shaped by the influence of others

The reality of this earliest phase of Moses' life is that much of it is shaped by decisions that lie entirely in the hands of other people.

In the summer of 2020, one of the guests on my podcast was Dave Burke. Dave lives in the North of England where he runs training in mental health first aid. Previously he served for several decades in church leadership in various parts of England. I think it's fair to

---

[13] Boers, *Servants and Fools*, p14.

say that Dave would describe himself theologically as a conservative, Free Church guy.

Which means that labyrinths would not normally have tended to be part of his expression of spirituality.

Nonetheless, Dave told me about an experience he had of walking through a labyrinth. He was visiting a retreat centre that was run by a couple of northern Anglican dioceses. The retreat centre had a labyrinth.

He admitted that his initial reaction was to think, 'What on earth is that for?' But he decided to walk the labyrinth, and as he did, he would try to remember everyone who had had an influence on him. It took a while. Every few feet he would recall his list of influencers in chronological order. By the time he got to the end of the labyrinth, he had a list of easily thirty people who had influenced him.[14]

I don't think we necessarily need to walk through a labyrinth to come up with a list of people upon whose shoulders we have climbed, or who have helped to steer us along the way, though if you have a labyrinth nearby, you may want to give it a try.

I can certainly recall the influence of many people on my life.

The first Christians I ever met were my parents. Like Moses, I was born into a family of faith. My parents had been followers of Jesus before I was born, so church and faith were very much part of my upbringing. As my faith grew and my vocational direction crystallised, my parents provided encouragement, as well as the freedom to move

---

[14] www.yourleadershipjourney.net/2020/07/10/the-leadership-journey-podcast-dave-burke/ (accessed 15th February 2021).

in expressions of church that were a bit different from their own.

I had Sunday school teachers and Bible class leaders. I listened to large quantities of preaching, some of it memorable and some of it less so. As a teenager I was invited by an older member of our church fellowship to do some preaching of my own: my first effort, in a little Gospel Hall on the County Down coast, was truly pitiful (though I probably was unaware of how pitiful at the time), and I can only hope that I have improved. There were people whose preaching ministry nourished me and helped me to see the relevance of the Bible to real life. There were those who taught me how to study the Bible, or whose relationship with God inspired me. There were opportunities to get involved in aspects of Christian ministry and help to discern my calling.

Beyond that there have been those who have influenced me from afar, through their writing or through their public ministry (some of them I have since had the opportunity to meet). There have been church members who have helped sharpen my thinking or have encouraged, even goaded, me in my growth and development.

I cannot leave this without mentioning my wife, who has been a wonderful support and partner with me and has helped develop and hone some of my ministry skills: not least in her challenge for me to answer the 'so what?' question in my preaching.

Like Moses, none of us is likely to get far without the involvement of others. In a recent conversation with a friend – on the theme of humility – he told me that if his life was a film, the credit list would be long.

Nor was it simply in his earliest years that Moses benefited from the part others played. At various phases in his leadership, others had contributions to make – something we will explore in Chapter Four when we will reflect on the part played by Jethro. We do well to remember that lesson for ourselves.

Defining moments

But the story of Moses' formative years is not only the story of the influence of others. As significant as that influence was, there comes a time when we all need to take responsibility and begin to make our own life-shaping choices. As Moses faced a significant defining moment in the second half of Exodus 2, so it is that from time to time leaders encounter these defining moments and arrive at major turning points.

The defining moment for Moses came when he saw an Egyptian beating a Hebrew. Without really developing the idea, the text observes that the people whom Moses saw struggling with their hard labour were 'his own people' (Exodus 2:11). As if to underline the point, the same verse describes the unfortunate Hebrew who is being beaten by the Egyptian as 'one of [Moses'] own people'.

This is significant. For all the privilege of his royal upbringing, Moses had not forgotten who his own people actually were. He was a Hebrew, and not an Egyptian.

The story of Moses striking down the Egyptian leaves us with some questions. Was Moses right to do what he did? He was certainly motivated by a keen sense of justice: this was not the last time he would stand up for the weak. Had he assumed that his unique background left him ideally placed to be what the Hebrews needed? If so, whatever memo Moses thought he was reading had not been delivered to the Hebrews, or if it had, they had not read it.

Is it possible, as John Calvin believed, that Moses had found his calling? Interestingly, Stephen, in Acts 7:25, claims that Moses thought that the Hebrews would understand that God had sent him. In that case we might wonder if the fault lay with the Hebrews who refused to accept him. Or could it be that Moses was right about his calling but wrong about his timing and method?

Calvin actually suggested that Moses had been divinely inspired with courage to deal with the Egyptian: this, says Calvin, was his vocation, and he knew it. His fault lay in his lack of boldness.[15]

On the other hand, Desmond Alexander notes that even though he may have been well motivated, there is nothing to suggest that Moses' actions are intended to be a model to be followed.

> His own desire for secrecy underlines the inappropriateness of what he does. Had he believed that his action was morally defensible,

---

[15] John Calvin, *Harmony of the Law, Volume 1,*
www.ccel.org/ccel/calvin/calcom03/calcom03.iv.ii.ii.html?queryID=78
72545&resultID=114015 (accessed 26th January 2021).

he might have claimed the authority for doing so on the basis of being a member of Pharaoh's household.[16]

Whichever of the arguments persuades you, the fact is that Moses' grand gesture failed to win over the Hebrews and he had to go on the run. It would be forty years before he would see his people again.

It was a mess, and in the next chapter we will explore the phase into which it plunged Moses. But it was a defining moment, and one which the anonymous writer of Hebrews appears to have in mind when writing about Moses' life-changing choice to identify with the Hebrews.

> By faith Moses, when he had grown up, refused
> to be known as the son of Pharaoh's daughter.
> He chose to be ill-treated along with the people
> of God rather than to enjoy the fleeting pleasures
> of sin.
> (Hebrews 11:24-25)

Moses' choice involved turning down the opportunity to enjoy 'the treasures of Egypt'; in their place, he would accept disgrace 'for the sake of Christ' (Hebrews 11:26). The author of Hebrews offers no criticism of his action: it was 'by faith' that Moses had made this choice (v24).

While it may well be true that significant elements of our lives are shaped by the decisions of others, leaders can expect that their leadership journey will toss up some defining moments when they need to make their mind up about their identity and the direction of their life.

---

[16] Alexander, *Exodus*, p67.

I'm not particularly into musical theatre in general, but I have watched the musical adaptation of Victor Hugo's *Les Misérables* on several occasions. It is full of powerful and poignant moments. There is the old priest who forgives Jean Valjean for exploiting his hospitality to steal from him: his redemptive act sets up Valjean's new life. There is the dramatic suicide of Inspector Javert, who has been let off the hook by Valjean but whose world has been so destabilised by this act of mercy that he cannot go on living. There is the moving moment at the end of Valjean's life when he is reunited with Cosette and Marius.

And there is a dramatic scene where Valjean, now a successful factory owner known as Monsieur Madeleine, realises that someone else has been mistaken for him and is on trial. To say nothing would condemn an innocent man, but to reveal his true identity would put the livelihood of his workers at risk.

In one of the show's many memorable moments, he weighs it all up (in a song – remember, it's a musical) before deciding to come clean and announce that he is indeed Jean Valjean. It's a defining moment.

Simply put, although in themselves they may be far from simple, and may involve anguished choices, defining moments are those moments that force us to decide who we are and what we stand for.

Who are you? Why are you here? What really matters? Why should you choose this path and not another? Why turn down some opportunities and accept others? Why should you draw a line here and not there?

These are vital questions for anyone to ask, never mind leaders.

The answers will not always make sense to other people. Why should someone turn down the prospect of a well-paid job to lose themselves as a missionary in some far-flung corner of the world, or because they know that the job may require choices that will conflict with their deepest convictions? Why would you turn your back on a comfortable existence to give your life in the service of people who have nothing of material value to give you in return? At various times we will need to 'nail our colours to the mast', perhaps when our colours are not in fashion. It's part of deciding who we are.

Even though the outcome of Moses' action was far from what he had envisaged, he had nonetheless marked a significant stage in his journey: he was a Hebrew, and these were his people. Moses had made a life-shaping decision about his identity.

It would be another forty years before it all really began to take shape; first, he had to spend time in the wilderness.

Questions for reflection

- Can you identify ways in which your circumstances have contributed to your leadership journey, in terms of both challenges and opportunities?

- Take some time to list the people who have most influenced you in terms of your faith and your leadership.

- Can you recall a defining moment when you had to decide what you and your leadership stood for?

2
Wise Leaders Learn to Navigate the Desert

Moses fled and became an exile in the land of Midian.
(Acts 7:29, ESV)

Several years ago, authors Warren Bennis and Robert Thomas set out to explore the influence of era in the development of leaders. While they discovered some key differences between the two generations of leaders they explored (they affectionately named them 'Geeks' and 'Geezers'), they were struck by the fact that everyone, regardless of their generation, had gone through some kind of intense, transformational experience. Bennis and Thomas decided to call these experiences 'crucibles'.[17]

The crucibles they discovered were by no means one-size-fits-all. For one person it might be spending sixteen years in a foreign prison, for another, the experience of

---

[17] Their work was the reference point for my own work on 'crucibles', mentioned in the introduction.

climbing a mountain. A crucible, they say, 'is an almost infinitely elastic term that is ultimately defined by the person transformed by it'.[18]

In a subsequent book,[19] Robert Thomas went on to define three types of crucible that a leader might expect to encounter during the course of a career. The first, which he called 'new territory', often relates to the early stage of a career and involves facing the new and the unknown. The second, 'reversal', is more often located in the middle of a career and may involve loss or failure. The third, 'suspension', involves some kind of break from previously familiar routines: these are times when leaders are challenged to clarify their personal sense of mission.

Thomas' concept of suspension has echoes of what Christian writers Robert Clinton and Shelley Trebesch refer to as 'isolation'.[20] In ministry terms, they're referring to a season in which a leader is set aside from normal ministry or leadership involvement. As with Thomas' experiences of suspension, isolation is a season that calls for an evaluation: for the Christian leader it's an evaluation of life and ministry, and of the leader's relationship with God.

Isolation is a form of wilderness, or desert. As Trebesch comments, 'over the many centuries of Christian

---

[18] Warren Bennis and Robert Thomas, *Geeks and Geezers: How Era, Values, and Defining Moments Shape Leaders* (Boston, MA: Harvard Business School Press, 2002), p96.

[19] Robert Thomas, *Crucibles of Leadership: How to Learn from Experience to Become a Great Leader* (Boston, MA: Harvard Business Press, 2008).

[20] Clinton, *The Making of a Leader*; Trebesch, *Isolation*.

spirituality, words such as "desert" and "wilderness" have been used to describe one's spiritual condition'.[21]

Moses' wilderness years

It is to the wilderness that we follow Moses in this chapter. His escape from Egypt took him into obscurity in Midian. While the biblical text gives few narrative details about Moses' years between the ages of forty and eighty, I think those four decades carry important lessons for navigating desert experiences.

Moses hardly expected to find himself living in the anonymity of the Midianite desert, especially given his high-flying Egyptian upbringing. Yet it was in Midian that he spent these middle years of his life. He met and married Zipporah, with whom he had two sons, and who would eventually become the fourth woman to preserve his life. Her father would also play an important role as a helpful source of practical advice.

Domestic blessings notwithstanding, this stage of Moses' life must have seemed odd for someone who was so passionate about the liberation of his people, not to mention the fact that it was arguably an unusual shift in career direction for such a well-educated future leader. The only hint as to his career path in Midian comes in the reference to him tending the flocks of his father-in-law: later he would shepherd God's people (Psalm 77:20).

No doubt there were significant lessons on wilderness survival that Moses would learn during his middle forty

---

[21] Trebesch, *Isolation*, p9.

years that would be of great value in his leadership years. How do you recognise a poisonous snake? Where is the best place to find water? While his forty years as an Egyptian prince would have contributed much to Moses' ability to think and to organise, shepherding in the Midianite wilderness would have helped round out his education.

Nonetheless, there must have been something profoundly disorientating about the change of situation. He'd gone from being a prince in the palace – Flavius Josephus, the Jewish historian, even suggests that Moses led Egyptian troops to victory over Ethiopian forces[22] – to being a shepherd, a profession that was despised among the Egyptians.

Over time, as we shall see, the wilderness years appear to have stripped Moses of his leadership aspirations and left him content to settle for a quiet existence in obscurity.

Wilderness can do that to a person.

In contrast, Norman Cohen makes the following more positive suggestion:

> Often, it is the kind of experience that Moses has in Midian that prepares a person to become a leader. Taken out of a familiar world and immersed in an altogether different one, a leader

[22] See Flavius Josephus, *Antiquities of the Jews*. Available online at penelope.uchicago.edu/josephus/ant-2.html (accessed 27th January 2021).

is forced to adapt and learn, to respond to all kinds of people.[23]

Before we attempt to make some specific observations about this middle period in Moses' life, I'd like us to step back for a moment and take a tour of some wider biblical background, for Moses' Midianite years are not the only wilderness experience in Scripture.

Wilderness in the Bible

Words for wilderness occur on almost 300 occasions in our Scriptures. An entire book is given over to wilderness: what our English Bibles refer to as the book of Numbers tends to be known in Hebrew as 'In the Wilderness', named from words that occur in the opening verse. At times, the biblical wilderness is marked by the apparent absence of God. For example, the title attributed to Psalm 63 locates it during David's time in the Desert of Judah. Although David spent time in the desert on the run from Saul before becoming king, the reference to the king towards the end of the psalm suggests that his experience is more likely to be located during his exile from Jerusalem following the takeover by his son Absalom. Here is how the psalm begins:

> You, God, are my God,
> Earnestly I seek you;
> I thirst for you,

---

[23] Norman Cohen, *Moses and the Journey of Leadership* (Woodstock, VT: Jewish Lights, 2008), p14.

my whole being longs for you,
in a dry and parched land
where there is no water.
(Psalm 63:1)

In the 'crucible' interviews I mentioned in the introduction, two of the leaders referred specifically to what they called a 'dark night of the soul', alluding to the work of the sixteenth-century priest and mystic, John of the Cross.[24]

For one leader, it was triggered by an extended season of chronic illness. She was completely unable to work. It felt as though every piece of 'scaffolding' in her life had been removed. The scaffolding included her sense of call and her love of ministry. She described how what she did was 'integral to who [she] was'. It was in fulfilling her call that she found a deep sense of joy, and that had been removed, with no certain prospect that she would ever regain it. There was an inevitable fear of what would become of her, and the question, 'Well, why, Lord?'

The other referred to a crisis of faith which seemed like a 'theological dark night of the soul', a kind of theological wilderness.

Whether or not you have spent much time in literal deserts, if you're a leader, and if Shelley Trebesch is right, there is a fair chance that you will spend time in a metaphorical or spiritual desert – if you have not already been there. Trebesch suggests that more than 90 per cent

---

[24] St John of the Cross, *Dark Night of the Soul* (New York: Riverhead Books, 2002).

of leaders can expect to experience at least one season of isolation in their lives.

Yet, as we shall eventually see in the story of Moses, the wilderness can also be a place of encounter with God. Such was the experience of Hagar. Twice in Genesis Hagar finds herself in the wilderness, first when she runs away from her mistress, Sarah,[25] as their relationship falls apart when Hagar is pregnant by Abraham (Genesis 16), and then when she and her son are sent away by Abraham (Genesis 21). On both occasions God intervenes and the angel of the Lord speaks to her.

Much later in the biblical timeline, God announces through the prophet Hosea that He will lead Israel into the wilderness, where He will 'speak tenderly' to her (Hosea 2:14): wilderness can be a place of divine encounter.

The wilderness wandering of Israel

I know I'm jumping ahead in terms of the chronology of Moses' story, and the chapter will get back to his middle years, but any wider reflection on the theme of wilderness needs to include Israel's journey to the Promised Land. First, they find themselves in the Desert of Sin on leaving Egypt and before reaching Sinai, the place of the covenant. Then, and for a prolonged period of time, they wander in the desert as a result of their disobedience and failure to trust God's ability to complete what He had started and allow them to take possession of Canaan.

---

[25] Sarah is initially referred to as Sarai (including in Genesis 16), and Abraham as Abram. For the sake of simplicity I have chosen to refer to each of them by their more familiar name.

If the wilderness can be portrayed both as a place where God seems to be absent and as a place where He can be encountered, another of its contrasts is seen in the way that for Israel it was both a place of fear at what appeared to be lacking and the place where they experienced the faithful provision of God. In Deuteronomy 29:5 Moses reminds Israel that during forty years of wandering, somehow their clothes have not worn out on them, nor have their sandals worn off their feet. While they have lacked the normal food supply, God has provided for them. In so doing, God has shaped the wilderness to function as a place of testing and learning, an extended education whose aim is to cultivate reliance on Him.

Think about the manna, the Old Testament equivalent of 'Give us today our daily bread' (Matthew 6:11). Scripture provides a varied assessment of the manna. From the account of its divinely ordained provision in Exodus 16 to its description as 'the grain of heaven' and 'the bread of angels' in Psalm 78:24-25, this was clearly a gift from God. Mysteriously, there was always just enough, but enough only for one day: try storing up a few days' supply, and you were likely to find it infested by maggots. The only exception was on the day before Sabbath when you could collect a double supply. If you forgot, you would go hungry on the Sabbath, because that was the one day in the week that none of it appeared.

There was something about the daily (not weekly or monthly) nature of the supply that was designed to inculcate a sense of trust and dependence on the part of the Israelites. 'He humbled you,' said Moses, 'causing you to hunger and then feeding you with manna, which neither you nor your ancestors had known, to teach you that man does not live on bread alone but on every word that comes from the mouth of the LORD' (Deuteronomy 8:3). Every morning that they went to gather manna – manna that had not been there the night before – was a reminder to them of their vulnerability (what if something happened and no manna had appeared?), of their utter dependence on God, and of God's faithfulness.

Perhaps unsurprisingly, however, while forty years of manna represented a remarkable provision (it stopped once the people were installed in the Promised Land and began to taste its food), some of the group eventually decided that they missed Egyptian cuisine and that they had had enough of the manna, leading to wailing on the part of the people and a leadership crisis for Moses (Numbers 11).

Jesus in the wilderness

There are clear echoes of Israel's story in Matthew's account of the series of temptations faced by Jesus at the start of His public ministry. Fresh from His baptism and the affirmation of His Father's love, Jesus found Himself in the wilderness (*eremos*), where the devil tempted Him. For Jesus, as had been the case for Israel, the wilderness became a place of testing. However, where Israel had failed to trust, Jesus submitted to His Father. He refused to use His power to take things into His own hands when He was hungry. He refused to engage in what would have been a publicity stunt. And He refused to give His worship to the tempter, even if to do so may have seemed like a shortcut to glory (Matthew 4:1-11).

But the wilderness was not only a place of testing; it was also a place of encounter. Not only do the Gospel writers talk about Jesus being 'led ... into the wilderness to be tempted' (Matthew 4:1), but they also note that there were times when He chose to spend time in the *eremos* as part of His practice of personal prayer. Luke tells us that it was His regular practice (Luke 5:16), while Mark notes an occasion when He sought out a deserted place 'while it was still dark' (Mark 1:35). This was no accidental add-on for Jesus in His public ministry: it was a priority.

Shelley Trebesch, mentioned earlier, suggests that while there are forms of isolation that are involuntary, such as those caused by illness, there are also times when isolation is chosen voluntarily by a leader.[26] For example, a leader may choose to step away from ministry to pursue further training or in order to seek renewal. This is wilderness, not experienced as a place of chaos but actually a place where chaos might be tamed and we might, like Hagar, meet with God. As Jewish author Erica Brown writes, 'what matters most can only be truly discovered where there are few distractions'.[27]

Back to Moses

With all of that wider reflection on the theme of wilderness in mind, we get back to the story of Moses, the fugitive.

---

[26] Trebesch, *Isolation*, pp30-34.
[27] Erica Brown, *Leadership in the Wilderness: Authority and Anarchy in the Book of Numbers* (Jerusalem: Maggid, 2013, Kindle Edition), loc.1172.

What are we to make of these forty years of Midianite exile[28] in Moses' life? What lessons can we draw? I want to make five observations about Moses in the desert.

Unanticipated circumstances

Picture Moses sitting by the well in Midian (Exodus 2:15): it's a serious understatement to say that this is not where he expected to be at this point in his life. Not only had he been forced to flee the place of his upbringing, but also an act of defiance that he thought might have led to the Hebrew slaves recognising him as their rescuer had blown up in his face.

We can only wonder at the kinds of questions that might have run through his mind as he sat by the well. What about the God whose story his mother may have told him as a young boy? Was He not pleased that Moses had opted to identify with His oppressed people rather than follow the much less risky path of enjoying his privilege as an Egyptian? Should he have adopted a more subtle approach to helping the Hebrews? Could he not have influenced policy from the inside? Why had the Hebrews not been prepared to accept him? Might they not have been grateful that at last someone had been prepared to see their plight and stand up for them?

His eventual encounter with God – some forty years later – would reveal the scars of his rejection: why would he go back to people who had previously been so quick to

---

[28] The ESV translates Stephen's description in Acts 7 of Moses' status in Midian as 'exile' (v29) and in so doing evokes another significant biblical theme.

close the door to him? What guarantee was there that they would listen this time?

Instead of living as a privileged and well-educated Egyptian, Moses found himself as an outsider. It must have been odd for someone described in Scripture as 'mighty in his words and deeds' (Acts 7:22, ESV) to be herding sheep, especially when he had had visions of himself as a leader.

If it's true, as we saw in Chapter One, that we don't get to choose the circumstances of our birth, it's also true that the course of our lives doesn't always follow our plan or our timetable. None of us can predict the unexpected twists and turns of our life. At the micro level, how often has a cancelled appointment or a flat tyre reminded us that we can't even control the way a morning will go? In the bigger picture, who could have predicted the events of recent years? One of the powerful lessons of Covid-19 has to be the reminder that we are not in control. James was right when he warned about the fragility of the plans of confident businessmen (James 4:13-15).

How many of us can say that life has turned out exactly as we had planned it, or that we are exactly where we thought we would be at this point? How many leaders have discovered that what they imagined would be the dream career path has proved to be anything but? How many pastors or ministers have arrived at a new post, convinced that they are God's guaranteed instrument of unbroken blessing, only to find, like Moses, that not everyone shares their optimism? How often has a new minister attempted to resolve a longstanding church issue, only to find themselves on the outside as old rivalries are set aside and former opponents turn on the usurper?

In his book *A Praying Life*, Paul Miller describes the gap that exists between hope and reality: he pictures this gap as a 'desert'.[29] It's a gap, according to Miller, that we sometimes attempt to close with denial: it's a form of hope that fails to face reality. At other times we attempt to close the gap through determination, as though by force of will we will be able to fix the situation, though this can lead to despair.

> It's a short trip from determination to despair, where you realize that you aren't going to change the situation, no matter what you do. It hurts to hope in the face of continued failure, so you try to stop hurting by giving up hope.[30]

This leads us to a second observation: the desert is a place of abandoned dreams.

Abandoned dreams

Although the text offers us few narrative details about Moses' forty years in Midian, it's a worthwhile exercise to compare Moses at forty with Moses at eighty.

No doubt there is a contrast between the levels of energy and motivation experienced by most eighty-year-olds and what they experienced at forty. I say 'most' rather

---

[29] Paul Miller, *A Praying Life: Connecting with God in a Distracting World* (Colorado Springs, CO: NavPress, 2009), p180.
[30] Ibid, p182.

than all, as many of us probably know inspiring people who measure up favourably to the remarkable figure of Caleb who, as Scripture notes, was as strong and battle-ready at eighty-five as he had been at forty (Joshua 14:11). The driving vision for the planting of the church I pastored in Switzerland came from a retired missionary in his seventies. I think he would have approved of a friend of mine (also in his seventies) who much prefers to talk in terms of 'refirement' than retirement!

You cannot really miss the difference between Moses at eighty and Moses at forty. Rejection and failure followed by forty years in obscurity left him content to accept a quiet life, looking after sheep, instead of jumping at the opportunity to do what had been in his heart four decades previously. *Forget the Hebrews and leave me alone with these sheep!* What starts out with the appearance of humility ('Who am I?' (Exodus 3:11)) is shown to be a deep reluctance to follow God's call.

Moses the elder had lost his vision and passion. God was offering him something that he would previously have accepted with enthusiasm. For Moses, the wilderness had become a place, if not of despair, at least of abandoned dreams.

Dan Allender's *Leading With a Limp* is an exploration of ways that leaders face some of the challenges of leadership, such as complexity or exhaustion. In discussing the exhaustion that comes from busy disillusionment, Allender reflects on the story of Moses and his time in the desert:

> Before he led a nation, he wandered in Midian
> for forty years and tended sheep. Our days spent

in the desert may be shorter, but they will be no less agonizing because they are a season of death. A leader's dreams must die if a deep soul is to be born. Idealism may get us into the fray, but it is the loss of all we cherish that begins to form in us a heart capable of leading others reluctantly and humbly.[31]

If Allender is right, the leader who has sat down by their well, confused and disappointed that their leadership has not accomplished what they thought it might, may begin to see their exhausted disillusionment as some kind of gift. Painful as that disillusionment may be, it might just prove to be the pathway that allows the leader to press the reset button and give space for God to work.

How remarkable – certainly by our reckoning – that God would choose a disillusioned eighty-year-old shepherd who wanted nothing more than the comfort of the familiar, instead of choosing a forty-year-old prince, full of passion and vision.

Unexpected allies

So far, we have construed the elements of Moses' Midianite desert experience as largely negative. He found himself somewhere he never expected to be, doing something he never expected to be doing, and after forty years he had lost his dream. But the wilderness was not all about loss. He gained a family.

---

[31] Dan Allender, *Leading With a Limp: Turning Your Struggles into Strengths* (Colorado Springs, CO: WaterBrook Press, 2006), p133.

It turns out that there was Old Testament precedent to sitting by a well.

Genesis 24 tells the story of Isaac and Rebekah. An ageing Abraham dispatched his servant (presumably Eleazar of Damascus) to find an appropriate bride for his son. It was as he waited by a well, praying for a sign, that the servant met Rebekah.

If it's true that history doesn't quite repeat itself but certainly rhymes, then we can be forgiven a degree of déjà vu in Genesis 29. This time the traveller was Jacob, Isaac's son, and it was by a well that he first met Rachel, a shepherdess who stole his heart and became one of his two wives.

With those incidents in mind, perhaps we're not entirely surprised by what happens as Moses sat down beside the well in Midian. I should add, in the interest of correct biblical application, as well as the avoidance of disappointment, that there is no guarantee that a single young man (or woman, for that matter) only needs to sit by a well in order to find their future spouse!

However, it worked for Moses.

As with his killing of the Egyptian, we see something of Moses' passion for justice as he intervened to scatter the shepherds who had attempted to prevent the seven shepherd girls (remember Rachel) who had appeared to water their father's flock (Exodus 2:15-17).

There is a homely touch of detail in the fact that, despite his help, for which the seven shepherdesses were doubtless grateful, Moses was left to fend for himself, without even the offer of a simple supper. After their father's intervention, Moses moved in and married one of the seven, Zipporah, who became the mother of his sons, Gershom and Eliezer. Some forty years later (Exodus 4) she became the fourth woman to save Moses' life in the 'bridegroom of blood' incident (v25). We hear very little more about her after this: chapter 18 notes that Moses had sent her back to her father, along with their two sons, Gershom and Eliezer,[32] and the reader is left wondering about the extent of Moses' engagement in family life.[33]

The same chapter that talks about Zipporah returning to her father also recounts a further incident involving him. The occasion was a family visit to see Moses. It was a good catch-up and the text says that Jethro was pleased to hear about 'the good things the LORD had done for Israel in rescuing them' from Egypt (v9): how affirming it must have been for Moses to have his father-in-law listen with such genuine interest to the story of God's work in his new leadership task.

We will say more in Chapter Four about the advice he gave to Moses – it was both wise and helpful – but for now we note just how important he became in the life of his son-in-law.

Reggie McNeal describes Jethro as 'the key male figure in Moses' midlife'. It's an astute observation. Was Jethro in fact the father that Moses never really had? We know he was nursed by his mother, but his natural father

---

[32] The names of both sons were comments on Moses' circumstances. Gershom could be translated as 'stranger there', while Eliezer means 'My God is helper'.
[33] Jewish tradition suggests that such was the intensity of his prophetic ministry, Moses later divorced his wife. The price paid by Zipporah, in losing her husband, thus allowed the Jews to have the leadership of Moses.

disappears from the early narrative, and we know nothing about his relationship with his adoptive father, assuming he had one. As McNeal reflects on the role Jethro played, he makes this wider observation, which I think bears repeating:

> The recounting of leaders' life journeys usually turns up a Jethro or two. These individuals are God's gifts to the leader to provide extraordinary affirmation, encouragement, and guidance. They frequently, but not always, arise from outside the family system. They typically surface during times of the leader's self-doubt and at points when the leader's life mission is crystallizing. These God-sent Jethros offer almost unconditional acceptance of the leader, yet they maintain an accountability of presence that implicates itself into the leader's choices.[34]

An obvious question for us is whether we notice or make room for the Jethro figures in our own leadership journeys, for we could probably all do with one. Beyond that, not least for some of us who are older, the challenge is to be that kind of spiritual father figure. How many younger leaders are looking for spiritual mothers and fathers?

So for all its challenges, Moses' wilderness throws up unexpected and unlikely allies.

---

[34] Reggie McNeal, *A Work of Heart: Understanding How God Shapes Spiritual Leaders* (San Francisco, CA: Jossey-Bass, 2000, Kindle Edition), loc.246.

Honest realisation

As we have noted, it's during this time that Moses had a son whom he named Gershom, a name that evokes the idea of being a foreigner.

When we lived in Switzerland, we became familiar with the idea of TCKs, or 'third culture kids'. These are children of expatriates who grow up between two cultures – the culture of their parents and the culture of the country in which they live. They have been described as 'global nomads' and 'cultural chameleons',[35] and while their upbringing has undoubted advantages in an interconnected world, some of them may feel that they don't fully belong anywhere.

In naming his son, Moses was acknowledging the issue of his own identity and the reality of his situation. He was living in Midian and apparently looked like an Egyptian, but was actually a Hebrew. Erica Brown observes that 'with each utterance of his child's name, he affirmed his status in the world as he experienced it. He belonged nowhere. He belonged to no one.'[36]

Part of what the wilderness does is reveal the reality of what is going on in our hearts. That's how it was with Israel: as Deuteronomy puts it, God led them in such a way as to test them in order to know what was in their hearts (Deuteronomy 8:2). At their core, were they

---

[35] See the discussion in Anna Dillon, and Ali Tabassim, 'Global Nomads, Cultural Chameleons, Strange Ones or Immigrants? An Exploration of Third Culture Kid Terminology with Reference to the United Arab Emirates', *Journal of Research in International Education* 18, No 1 (April 2019), pp77–89.

[36] Brown, *Leadership in the Wilderness*, loc.1641.

obedient or not? Sadly, they struggled to live in faithful obedience. The wilderness laid bare what was going on in the deep places of their being, just as Midian brought Moses to an honest realisation of his struggle of identity and belonging.

It's not always easy for leaders to admit the reality of a wilderness situation, to admit that things have not gone according to plan (at least, the leader's plan), to admit that all is not well. At times it seems more spiritual and more faith-filled to put a brave face on things. Some of us have bought into the idea that we must always be seen to be leading with our best foot forward. Much as we might claim that 'it's OK not to be OK', as the popular saying goes, perhaps we don't really believe it, or at least we don't really believe it applies to leaders. Certainly when it comes to mental health, there are still some taboos, and there is still a belief that Christian leaders should somehow be exempt.

Yet leaders – and their families – live in the same broken world as everyone else, and they are not exempt from experiencing difficulty or disappointment.

Faced with the disappointment of unexpected circumstances and the loss of a dream, it's easy, as Paul Miller says, to default to some form of denial.[37] In naming his son, Moses was acknowledging the reality of his circumstances.

---

[37] See Miller, *A Praying Life*, p181.

Transforming encounter

It was in the desert that Moses encountered God.

I've had the opportunity to visit Israel twice. On both occasions I've spent time with a wonderful Jewish guide called Josh. One evening, as he returned our small group to our accommodation, he asked us a question that was intended to prepare us for the next day's excursion, an excursion to the desert: 'Do you go into the desert to stay in the desert, or do you go into the desert in order to return?'

It's a very insightful question. Is the desert meant to be a place of escape, a way of getting beyond the corrupting influence of the city and what Christians have referred to as 'the world'? Or is the desert meant to offer a place of temporary retreat, somewhere to prepare for mission in the world?

For Moses, Midianite obscurity was temporary – albeit spanning four decades – but exile would not be the final word on his story.

For as we have already seen, while the wilderness can be a place from which God seems to be absent, it is also a place where He can be encountered: and so it was for Moses. It was as he led his father-in-law's sheep in the desert that he met God and experienced the second significant turning point in his leadership journey, a turning point that would propel him into his life's main work.

We will explore what happened in his encounter with God in the next chapter, but before we go there, take a moment to reflect on the verbs that cluster in the closing verses of Exodus 2 (24-25):

- God *heard* the people's groaning;

- God *remembered* the covenant He had made with Abraham and the other patriarchs;

- God *looked* on His suffering people;

- God was *concerned* for them.

God had not forgotten His people. Nor had He forgotten Moses. A leader who is experiencing the wilderness of isolation can easily think that God must have forgotten. But the wonderful grace in Moses' story is that the edge of the desert – a place of unexpected and unsought circumstances, and a place of abandoned dreams – becomes a place to meet God and a place where life is rebooted.

Just as the bush that caught his attention and from which God speaks is burning but is not consumed, so Moses has survived exile. Disillusioned he may be, but God has work for him to do.

But first, Moses will have to get beyond his excuses.

Questions for reflection

- Have you ever experienced a sense of being in a wilderness: for example, when there has been a gap between what you had planned or hoped for and where you actually found yourself?

- The chapter mentioned Erica Brown's claim that 'what matters most can only be truly discovered where there are few distractions' (p52): to what extent do you seek to make intentional solitude a part of your life?

- Which of the five aspects of Moses' experience in Midianite exile most resonates with you?
    - Unanticipated circumstances
    - Abandoned dreams
    - Unexpected allies
    - Honest realisation
    - Transforming encounter

3

Wise Leaders Get Over Their Excuses

Please send someone else.
(Exodus 4:13)

If I were to offer an alternative title to this chapter, I think I might borrow from Stephen Covey's famous book[38] and call it *The Five Excuses of Highly Reluctant Leaders*.

So far we have followed Moses' formative years as he grew up between two cultures, with the earliest course of his life shaped by several women, including the daughter of the man who wanted him and all the other Hebrew baby boys wiped out. We've explored the middle years – his years of exile in the Midianite desert, an unexpected season which appears to strip him of his passion and vision, but during which he is not forgotten by God. Having allowed a forty-year-old Moses to flounder in his attempts to become a leader, God meets the chastened,

---

[38] Stephen R Covey, *The 7 Habits of Highly Effective People* (New York: Simon & Schuster, 1989).

eighty-year-old Moses and prepares to send him on a mission.

I suspect that, in normal circumstances, any of us wanting to recruit someone for the task that Moses was about to step into would be drawn more to a passionate forty-year-old than to an eighty-year-old whose ambitions did not seem to extend beyond the scope of a relatively obscure life in Midian. By this stage in his life we would imagine that the ship of a significant career had sailed.

But it is this Moses that God calls, and not the younger version.

Remarkable. Perhaps Moses had not been ready at forty, but why not choose another, more suitable forty-year-old rather than wait four decades and call someone whose more energetic days are presumably well behind him? That may be what we would have done, but the Lord has waited patiently as Moses' training and education have continued through a season of his life in which he could hardly have guessed that his most fruitful years were still ahead of him.

The angel of the Lord appears to him in a desert bush (Exodus 3:2), likely a wild acacia bush. Richard Bauckham makes this observation:

> Frequently in the early books of the Bible, when the figure of the Angel of the LORD appears, this angel is not just a messenger of God, like most angels, but virtually the presence of God himself

on earth. The angel's presence is God's presence;
what the angel says, God says.[39]

There are linguistic connections between the Hebrew for 'bush' and 'Sinai', reckoned by many scholars to be another name for what the opening verse of Exodus 3 refers to as 'Horeb, the mountain of God'. Not only is the Lord the God who will later reveal Himself in the terrifying majesty of fire on Mount Sinai (Exodus 19), but He also reveals Himself in fire in a humble desert shrub. In the burning bush the ordinary becomes extraordinary, and the ground that had previously been trampled by flocks and herds becomes holy.

First-class noticers

It was Moses' ability to notice something unusual that started him on this encounter with God. You would suspect that a smouldering bush in the desert was not uncommon: it's not hard to imagine that a shepherd may have lit a simple campfire to keep himself warm overnight, and when he moved on with his flocks, the embers of the fire remained. It must have happened all the time.

However, there was something different about this. Although the bush was burning, the fire did not consume it. That is what was unusual, and that is what led Moses to divert from his path: this unusual phenomenon needed a closer look.

---

[39] Richard Bauckham, *Who is God? Key Moments of Biblical Revelation* (Grand Rapids, MI: Baker Academic, 2020, eBook edition), p36.

To borrow from leadership scholar Warren Bennis, a leader is a 'first-class noticer'.[40] They have a capacity to notice things that other people miss. Perhaps that's part of the reason that some people never become truly effective leaders: they have never developed the capacity to notice what is out of the ordinary.

Aside from the leadership implications of this, there are spiritual implications: how many Christian leaders have not grown in their leadership because they have failed to pay attention to something that God intends them to pay attention to? How many leaders have never slowed down sufficiently to cultivate a sensitivity to those moments when God is speaking?

Perhaps one of the reasons we need to develop the skill of attentiveness is that God does not always raise His voice.

Generations after Moses, Elijah, another great figure in the story of Israel, also found himself on Mount Horeb. As Moses had previously done, Elijah had gone on the run, in his case from Queen Jezebel. After an initial stop-off when he was supernaturally provided for, he travelled to Horeb, where the Lord asked him to 'go out and stand on the mountain in the presence of the LORD, for the LORD is about to pass by' (1 Kings 19:11).

A fiercely powerful wind was followed by an earthquake, and then by a fire. The Lord – who had already demonstrated His power through fire in the confrontation on Carmel (1 Kings 18) – was in none of them. But 'after the fire came a gentle whisper' (19:12): God was now ready to speak to His weary prophet.

---

[40] Bennis and Thomas, *Geeks and Geezers*, p19.

If we only ever expect to hear God in the wind and the fire, we may miss His gentle whisper. And if our lives are filled with noise, a whisper is easy to miss.

Back to Moses: I doubt that he expected to hear God speak from the bush, but in noticing and being attentive to this unusual phenomenon, he was ready to hear Him when He did.

Called and commissioned

Having caught Moses' attention, God spoke to him, calling him twice by name. The dialogue that follows runs for two chapters in Exodus, and rabbinic tradition suggests that the episode may have occupied a full week. It is perhaps most remarkable for the ingenuity of Moses' excuses. Like Jeremiah, a later prophet in Israel's history, Moses was a hesitant spokesman who claimed that he was unable to speak with any degree of eloquence.

Perhaps his reluctance is understandable for someone who had endured a dramatic rejection four decades previously. However, even if we have a degree of sympathy for him, his concluding objection in chapter 4:13 ('Please send someone else') leaves us in no doubt about his fundamental reluctance to do what God was asking him.

Experiences such as that of Moses in this story or, later, of Isaiah, Peter or Saul/Paul, whereby the normal course of life is interrupted by a call to 'full-time ministry', have shaped many Christians' understanding of what it means to be called. It's not uncommon for Christian leaders, not least those in vocational church ministry or engaged in mission, to talk about the details of their experience of being called to what they are doing.

For some, the call has come about in the context of a dramatic experience such as an emotional response to a challenging message at a Christian event. For others, it's been more of an inner struggle to come to terms with a growing conviction that there is something specific that God wants them to do with their life. Some talk about a sense of God speaking through a specific passage of Scripture, and some talk about the part played by the advice of wise friends.

The task of discerning God's call, or trying to work out the specific will of God for their lives, has probably been a cause of angst for many zealous followers of Jesus. Allied to the question of finding 'the one' to marry (if marriage is in God's plan) is the question of whether there is a particular career or vocational track that God has mapped out: if we miss it, we may have to spend the rest of life living out 'plan B'.

Forty years ago, Garry Friesen challenged the common evangelical understanding of some of this in his book, *Decision-Making and the Will of God*. Friesen argued that while the idea of God's call is prominent in the New Testament, its use in a vocational sense is more limited. He questioned what he saw as an exegetically dubious and overly subjective sense of call and thought it was a flimsy anchor on which to rely for stability in 'the heavy seas of Christian ministry'.[41]

---

[41] Garry Friesen, with J Robin Maxson, *Decision-Making and the Will of God: A Biblical Alternative to the Traditional View* (Portland, OR: Multnomah, 1980), p320.

Even if Garry Friesen may have tossed a few babies out with the bathwater, there is certainly scope for us to reconsider some aspects of the traditional evangelical understandings of calling. For example, while there is doubtless much to learn from the biblical accounts of dramatic, life-altering encounters, should we necessarily assume that the absence of a burning bush or a road to Damascus invalidates a leader's ministry? Should we all stand around doing nothing, waiting for writing in the sky (or some kind of equivalent), as though the absence of such writing means that God has nothing for us to do?

Similarly, although on more than one occasion I believe I have sensed God speaking very specifically into a particular situation through a particular Bible verse, we need to have a degree of caution when it comes to overly subjective readings of Scripture that completely ignore the original context and intent.

We ought also to consider rebalancing some of the individualism that's involved in seeking to discern God's call. At times the New Testament is as concerned about the role of others in helping to call people into leadership and ministry as it is about an individual Damascus Road experience. It's striking that the initiative for Barnabas and Saul's first missionary venture came not simply from a personal and subjective sense of call, but within the context of a ministry team seeking God together: it was then that the Holy Spirit spoke (Acts 13:2). In addition, where was Timothy's personal sense of call in Acts? He appears to have been selected by Paul, presumably on the recommendation of the leaders of his church (Acts 16:2). Is there a contemporary challenge for church leaders to be more proactive in encouraging people into leadership?

Of course, none of this is to say that there is no degree of subjectivity or that there should be no individual sense of conviction involved in discerning a call. However, there are dimensions to the concept that some of us may have either underplayed or overplayed.

In his book *The Call*, Os Guinness challenges those who limit the call to what he calls 'the fallacy of the contemporary Protestant term *full-time Christian service*'.[42] The call is much more comprehensive.

> Calling is the truth that God calls us to himself so decisively that everything we are, everything we do, and everything we have is invested with a special devotion and dynamism lived out as a response to his summons and service.[43]

Guinness goes on to distinguish between what he calls an 'ordinary' call and a later, 'special' call. The latter comes about when an individual receives a specific, supernatural communication from God, leading them to a specific task or mission. It contrasts with a more 'ordinary' sense of life purpose in response to God's call to follow Him, a calling whose implications are to be lived out even if there is no direct, even supernatural, communication from God about a special calling.

And that is helpful. No follower of Jesus is without a call. All of us are called to follow Christ, to belong to Him,

---

[42] Os Guinness, *The Call: Finding and Fulfilling God's Purpose for Your Life* (Nashville, TN: Thomas Nelson, 2018), p62.
[43] Guinness, *The Call*, p5.

to be like Him. Any particular sense of call to a specific task or role, even to a specific place, ought to be a subset of that fundamental call. As a friend once put it to me, 'The question is: am I being faithful where I am? Not: am I in the right place?'

Before leaving this discussion of calling, I should mention the Quaker writer Parker Palmer, who uses the term 'vocation'. He notes Buechner's wonderful definition of vocation as 'the place where your deep gladness meets the world's deep need', and adds a definition of his own.

> Vocation at its deepest level is, 'This is something I can't not do, for reasons I'm unable to explain to anyone else and don't fully understand myself but that are nonetheless compelling.'[44]

There is something very powerful about the concept of something that 'I can't not do'. As Paul put it, 'Woe to me if I do not preach the gospel!' (1 Corinthians 9:16).

As for Moses, once God had told him to remove his sandals and described who He is – the God of Moses' father and the God of the patriarchs – He gave him an initial summons that had two elements:

- Moses was to go to Pharaoh;
- Moses was to bring God's people out of Egypt.

---

44 Parker J Palmer, *Let Your Life Speak: Listening for the Voice of Vocation* (San Francisco, CA: Jossey-Bass, 2000), p25.

The summons is rooted in God's concern for His people's misery. By now it had been eighty years since the birth of Moses during Pharaoh's campaign of infanticide. God had seen Israel's misery and heard their cries and had come to rescue them from Egypt ('the narrow places'[45]) to bring them to Canaan, 'a good and spacious land' (Exodus 3:8).

The reluctant leader

Immediately we can imagine some potential concerns for Moses. If he was worried that he might still be on a 'most wanted' list, even after so many years, God allayed those fears by telling him that the people who had wanted to kill him were now dead (Exodus 4:19). As for leading God's people, his previous attempt had ended in failure: what guarantee was there it would go any better this time? That's a theme to which Moses would turn and which would become a point of contention in his debate with God.

One of the pitfalls of leadership is what I would call 'David Moyes syndrome'. Without getting into too much obscure detail, Moyes was manager at English football club Everton for eleven years. While some Everton purists with a rich sense of history will point to his lack of trophies and will disagree with me, I prefer to think that his tenure was moderately successful as he helped a historic club with a proud record that had come uncomfortably close to relegation establish itself at the higher end of the league table. After eleven years he left to succeed Sir Alex

[45] The Hebrew word for Egypt echoes the word for 'narrow places': see Cohen, *Moses and the Journey of Leadership*, p5.

Ferguson as manager at Manchester United. He was sacked from this position after ten months.

No doubt there are many complex factors that combine to explain the failure of this career step, but it seems as though for every leader who manages to successfully negotiate the challenge of ever-bigger tasks and increasing responsibility, there are others who find that they have taken one step too many and have stretched themselves beyond their capacity. If you're a cautious type, perhaps it's better to stay put and let someone else take on the challenge, especially if you are eighty years old and you've grown comfortable in the obscurity of the wilderness.

While we may instinctively be a little suspicious of reluctant leaders (if they don't really want to be here, doing this, then make way for someone else), our fears may be misplaced. Writing about US President Eisenhower, author Sam Walker suggested that one of the reasons for his success was his disinclination to seek the presidential office.[46] In a not dissimilar vein, Shlomo Ben-Hur and Karsten Jonsen warn that 'when ambition is the motivating factor, the leader is not a true leader, but a commander'.[47]

Moses was a reluctant leader whose ambition had evaporated. His reluctance is demonstrated in his excuses, his five objections to God's call.

---

[46] Sam Walker, www.wsj.com/articles/the-eisenhower-code-happy-to-serve-reluctant-to-lead-1544191201 (accessed 8th October, 2021).
[47] Shlomo Ben-Hur and Karsten Jonsen, 'Ethical Leadership: Lessons from Moses', *Journal of Management Development*, Volume 31, No 9, 2012, p966. Used with permission.

Excuse #1: Who am I?

'Who am I?' is a reasonable question to ask when you're confronted with a significant task, and at first reading it's hard to fault Moses for asking it. Perhaps he'd become too settled in his new identity as a nomadic shepherd to think that he'd carry much clout with Pharaoh. Egyptian royalty was unlikely to have much time for Midianite shepherds (even if Moses' rash act of forty years previously had been forgotten). Besides, leading a vast crowd of people on the kind of journey that was envisaged was a bit of a step up from herding sheep.

'Who am I …?' (Exodus 3:11).

Elsewhere in the Old Testament, David asked the same question on more than one occasion. First, in 1 Samuel 18:18, when Saul (albeit with dubious motives) appeared to offer him his daughter in marriage, David questioned his own significance and the significance of his family. The dignity of being the king's son-in-law was beyond him.

Second, and more significant in how it relates to Moses' question, is how David answered the Lord on hearing His promise to establish his royal line. 'Who am I, Sovereign LORD,' he asked, 'and what is my family, that you have brought me this far?' (2 Samuel 7:18).

What had started out as a proposal from David to build a house (temple) for the Lord had become a promise from the Lord to establish the house (family line) of David, and David was struck by a deep sense of grateful humility.[48]

---

[48] See also 1 Chronicles 29:14, in the context of David's prayer towards the end of his life.

In his excellent book on the subject, Ian Parkinson suggests that 'perhaps what most distinguishes Christian leadership from any other form of leadership is the understanding that it is received from God as a gift'.[49]

If he is right, then 'Who am I?' is exactly the right response for anyone who finds that God has entrusted them with the privilege of leadership and the responsibility for the well-being of others. Christian leadership is not intended to be an ego-booster, and something is amiss when Christian leaders lead with a sense of entitlement, and communicate the idea that the whole enterprise is about them.

Indeed, humility is a key, if a sometimes overlooked, indicator of growth in Christian character. God opposes proud people but is ready to pour grace into the life of a humble person (1 Peter 5:5). As Jesus said, 'all those who exalt themselves will be humbled, and those who humble themselves will be exalted' (Luke 18:14).

Yet, as is the case with other virtues, there are counterfeits.

There can be a false or overstated form of humility that leaves us so entrapped in 'worm theology' that we don't know what to do with a compliment. It may blind us to gifts that God has graciously and generously given us, and it may leave us reluctant to attempt to do anything for God lest we get carried away. At times it's fed by well-meaning folk who are reluctant to praise us out of a fear that we will be absorbed by pride and self-confidence and end up shipwrecked on the sidelines.

---

[49] Ian Parkinson, *Understanding Christian Leadership* (London: SCM Press, 2020), p252.

While we may be aware of plenty of people who think more highly of themselves than they ought, how many are there who think so lowly of themselves that they miss God's call on their lives? Rather than allowing God to work, this form of humility can – as in the case of Moses – be an excuse for dodging the call.

Moses was by no means done with his objections, but here is how God answered this first one:

> I will be with you. And this will be the sign to you that it is I who have sent you: when you have brought the people out of Egypt, you will worship God on this mountain.
> (Exodus 3:12)

Simply put, the question of Moses' fitness for the task was less significant than the fact that the God who was calling him promised to be with him.

It's intriguing that the confirming sign that God offered appeared to be in the future. Eventually Moses would be back at Horeb/Sinai, and once again he would have an encounter with God. When that happened, he would know that God had really sent him. For now, he had to trust the promise.

Excuse #2: Who are You?

With God having promised to be with him, thus setting aside the issue of Moses' fitness for the job, Moses started to think ahead, imagining the conversation with the Hebrews. Who is this God, anyway?

'I AM WHO I AM' (Exodus 3:14), or, as some scholars[50] prefer, 'I WILL BE WHAT I WILL BE'.

Richard Bauckham writes, 'what God says to Moses amounts to "I will be whoever I choose to be" or "I am free to be who I choose to be."'[51]

> In more technical language, we might say that God is utterly self-determining. He cannot be constrained by anything other than himself. He can say who he is and who he will be only by reference to himself, not by reference to anything else.[52]

Depending on the context, I might define myself as the son of my parents, the husband of my wife or the father of my children (it's interesting how these things shift as you get older, and now I have grandchildren!). God certainly described Himself in relation to the fathers of the Israelites (Exodus 3:6), but whether or not they had ever existed, God would still be God.

While at first His answers to Moses' question might appear somewhat evasive, as though he was refusing to be nailed down, God then named Himself as the LORD (verse 15; the Hebrew YHWH looks like a play on words with the verb 'I will be').[53] It's a name that, as Desmond Alexander observes, 'does not limit God's nature to any particular characteristic: he is what he is'.[54]

---

50 See the footnote in the NIV.

51 Bauckham, *Who is God?*, p42.

52 Ibid, p42.

53 Ibid, p43.

54 Alexander, *Exodus*, p91.

If we are correct in putting the emphasis more on the future than on the present tense – 'I WILL BE WHAT I WILL BE' – then God was promising to be with Moses and that He would be sufficient for everything that Moses and the Israelites would need. Not only would God be with Moses, but He would also be whatever He would be, without constraint or limitation.

If part of a leader's reluctance to respond to God's call results from issues around their own identity ('Who am I?'), it's also true that part of their reluctance may result from issues around questions of God's identity ('Who are You?').

Jesus told a story that we normally think of as the parable of the talents (Matthew 25:14-30). A man entrusted his servants with what the NIV translates as 'bags of gold'. To one servant he gave five bags, to another two and to a third, one. Eventually the master returned and asked the servants to account for what he had entrusted to them. The first two servants had doubled their master's investment and were suitably rewarded. The third servant had hidden his bag of gold in the ground.

His reasoning was his perceived harshness of the master.

Matthew Henry's comment on the third servant is astute.

> The spirit of a slave; I was afraid. This ill affection toward God arose from his false notions of him; and nothing is more unworthy of God, nor more hinders our duty to him, than slavish fear. This has bondage and torment, and is directly opposite to that entire love which the

> great commandment requires. Note, *Hard thoughts of God drive us from, and cramp us in his service.* Those who think it impossible to please him, and in [sic] vain to serve him, will do nothing to purpose in religion.[55]

What is our perception of the kind of God who calls us to serve Him in the exercise of the leadership that He has entrusted to us? Do we perceive Him as harsh and mean? If we do, we may well find that our service is slavish, fearful and even reluctant. However, if we perceive Him as gracious and generous, His grace and generosity are more likely to spill over into the way we follow Him and the way we lead.

Moses' journey was not simply about leadership: it was a journey in knowing God. As he led, he began to discover something of God's greatness and power (Deuteronomy 3:24). The most truly effective Christian leadership will come from those who are growing in their knowledge of God and growing in His grace. They know Him well enough to trust Him and they trust Him enough to lead boldly, knowing that He will be who He will be.

Excuse #3: What about them?

Despite God's extensive answer to his second question, and His promise that 'the elders of Israel will listen to you'

---

[55] Matthew Henry, *Matthew Henry Commentary on the Whole Bible*, www.biblestudytools.com/commentaries/matthew-henry-complete/matthew/25.html (accessed 11th November 2020), emphasis mine.

(Exodus 3:18), Moses had not finished. What would happen if, in fact, the people didn't believe him or listen to him, and instead were to question the legitimacy of his commission?

At this point, Moses' stubbornness was starting to emerge. Even though the Lord had told him that the elders would listen, Moses still questioned his likely reception (Exodus 4:1). Despite this emerging stubbornness, I wonder if a few of us might have a degree of sympathy for him. After all, he'd been here before and perhaps, even after forty years, the scars were still tender.

Our family once drove a large estate car. At the time we were living in an apartment block with an underground garage. There were two vehicle entrances: one involved going up a slight slope, the other involved going down. Residents had a key to operate the garage doors. One evening it had been raining and I was taking the downslope entrance to the garage. When I stopped at the top of the slope to turn the key and activate the door, there was a problem. For a moment the tyres refused to grip and the car slid towards the door. Thankfully it was just a moment and there was no crash, but the skid marks remained on the slope for years (they may still be there) as a reminder of the evening I might have crashed the car.

It's a trivial illustration, but it's a reminder that when things go wrong, the marks and scars can remain for a long time. Perhaps we've tried something once and it hasn't worked: why should we think it will work this time? I dare say there are quite a few church leaders who have had to listen to this objection.

Of course, you may already have realised that there is a mirror opposite to the excuse of 'we tried that before and it didn't work': it's the excuse of 'we've never tried that before, so we're not going to try it now'. Either way, nothing gets done as we settle for the comfort zone.

More painfully, though, when there has been personal rejection, the wounds may still be sensitive. We've attempted to lead these people before, but they wrote us off: why should we think they will accept us this time? How do you return to those who have rejected you? How do you go back to people who have already made it clear that they don't want you? I wonder how many pastors and ministers have come to dread church gatherings, including Sunday mornings, because they cannot erase the recollection of an angry phone call or a series of dismissive emails from a vocal section of the congregation.

At this point it sounds as though Moses was attempting to defend himself against what he thought would be an exercise in futility. But God was not really exploring his willingness to sign up as a casual volunteer: there was more to this call than that. And Moses appeared to be missing the point of God's promises: He *would* be with him, and the people *would* listen to him.

God's answer here was to equip Moses with three miraculous signs: one involved his staff, one involved his hand and one involved water from the Nile.

Let's think about the first sign for a moment.

I imagine that a shepherd's staff was as common in the desert as an umbrella in an Irish seaside resort in July (I am writing this on a very damp July afternoon in Ireland).

There would be nothing remarkable about it. It was simply an everyday piece of the shepherd's equipment.

Even if you and I are unlikely to be walking in the desert carrying a shepherd's staff, it's worth asking ourselves, 'What is that in your hand?' (Exodus 4:2). What ordinary and everyday aspect of your life might God want to infuse with His power? Maybe, like Moses, what you have in your hand represents a tool of your profession, or it's symbolic of a particular skill or ability you have.

God specialises in using the ordinary and the everyday.

In the Gospels, Jesus transformed the ordinary. Water was turned into wine. Bread and fish were multiplied to feed a crowd. Mud was used in the process of healing a blind man. A motley crew of fishermen and tax collectors was transformed, first as they spent time with Jesus, then (in Acts) through the gift of the Holy Spirit. Their transformation was such that they were accused of turning the world 'upside down' (Acts 17:6, ESV).

Paul, who came slightly later to the party, grasped the idea of God at work through the ordinary when he wrote about 'treasure in jars of clay' (2 Corinthians 4:7). He learned that there was something about the ordinariness of the jar that drew more attention to the treasure.

Just as God had transformed an ordinary shrub in the desert and had rendered the ground around it holy, so God transformed an ordinary shepherd's staff, turning it into a symbol of His power and authority.

From this point on, the staff (sometimes referred to as Aaron's staff, sometimes as the staff of God) took on a significant symbolic role in Moses' leadership. On nine further occasions the staff is associated with some kind of supernatural intervention, whether it was when it became a serpent at the start of the contest with the Egyptian magicians, dividing the Red Sea or bringing about victory (at the hands of Joshua) over Amalek. Sadly, the staff would also feature in the low point of Moses' ministry, when he would strike the rock at Meribah, a salutary tale that, among other things, illustrates an abuse of the power that God had put in Moses' hands: leaders beware![56]

Excuse #4: What about this?

Still Moses had not come to an end of his excuses. It's difficult not to see a degree of irony in his claim that he had 'never been eloquent' (Exodus 4:10). For someone who had never been eloquent, he demonstrated a remarkable ability to carry on a spirited debate with God: Pharaoh and the Israelites ought to be straightforward after this. In the New Testament, Stephen describes Moses as having been 'powerful in speech and action' (Acts 7:22).

Nonetheless, it had been some time since his prestigious Egyptian education. And what did Moses mean when he claimed to be 'slow of speech and tongue' (Exodus 4:10)? While there are various opinions as to the nature of Moses' speech issue, there is some evidence that he had a stammer. Later (Exodus 6:12, 30) Moses would once again raise with the Lord the issue of his speech. Why

---

[56] The incident with the magicians is in Exodus 7, the parting of the Red Sea in Exodus 14, and the battle with Amalek in Exodus 17. The rock-striking incident, which we will consider later in the book, comes in Numbers 20.

would someone like Pharaoh listen to someone like him who spoke with 'faltering [literally: uncircumcised] lips'?

As before, we may feel a degree of sympathy for him. A leadership task on this scale is a big ask for anyone, never mind someone who appears to lack what might seem to be one of the most important tools for the job.

Again God answered. He is sovereign over the physical conditions that might help or hinder His servants: Moses' task was to go, and the Lord would both help him to speak and teach him what to say: He would equip him for the task (Exodus 4:12).

Most of us probably have enough instinctive sense of hermeneutics to understand that when Paul wrote to his friends in Philippi about being able to do all things through Christ who gave him strength (Philippians 4:13), he did not have in mind someone attempting to run a marathon without training, or sight-reading a Beethoven piano sonata without having had a music lesson. He was reflecting on the range of circumstances he had experienced as a servant of God and acknowledging that whatever circumstances God permitted him to experience, Christ would give him the strength to live through them.

It seems that there had been times when he'd had plenty of material supplies to live on and there had been times when he'd gone hungry. But he'd learned the secret of being content either way, confident that Christ would give him the strength he needed.

So it is that Moses, about to be launched out on the adventure of leadership, needed to learn that God would equip him for the challenge to which He called him.

There is a popular statement – of the kind that fits well as an internet meme – whose original source I have not been able to identify: 'God does not call the equipped, he equips the called.' It's a helpful statement and would be an appropriate comment at this point in Moses' story and a pertinent word of encouragement to any leader battling their reluctance and the daunting nature of their task.

Excuse #5: What about someone else?

Finally Moses was out of excuses.

> Pardon your servant, Lord. Please send someone
> else.
> (Exodus 4:13)

However valid some of his objections may have been, the underlying reality is that Moses wanted someone else to do this.

God had been patient up to this point – He is 'slow to anger' (Exodus 34:6) – but now He was angry (Exodus 4:14). Reggie McNeal has noted the providences that had brought Moses to this point and uniquely equipped him for the task ahead of him. But here he was, ready to walk away.[57]

I listened recently to a talk about Barnabas and John Mark. The speaker pointed out something that I had never noticed. In the aftermath of the dramatic falling-out between Barnabas and Paul that's recounted in Acts 15:36-41, Barnabas took John Mark to Cyprus. Given that the

---

[57] McNeal, *A Work of Heart*, loc.284.

New Testament tells us that Barnabas was a Cypriot and that John Mark was his cousin, you could make the case that Barnabas was reintroducing John Mark to ministry by taking him back to a place which may have been more accessible to him than some of the less hospitable places he would have encountered with Paul, and after all, he seems to have managed fine in Cyprus previously (Acts 13).

If this is right, the episode tosses up the intriguing idea that the comfort zone may not always deserve its negative press: at times it can function as a place of restoration, a place where leaders are led by 'still waters' (Psalm 23:2, ESV) and have the opportunity to refresh their souls.

Be that as it may, how many leaders have found that the comfort zone has been too comfortable? They'd rather be left alone than accept the challenge of an assignment that God has prepared for them. How many have opted to potter about in the desert with a few sheep rather than become part of something that stretches beyond their narrowed horizons? In Moses' case, the comfort zone threatened to get in the way of his call, and he wanted to walk away. How ironic that the man who, forty years previously, believed he was God's chosen deliverer should now turn down that very same role.

God had still one more move to make. Aaron – who was already on the way to meet Moses – would make a good second-in-command (Exodus 4:14). Moses could tell him what to say and God would be with both of them.

Somehow that settled it for Moses. There was none of the 'Here am I. Send me!' of Isaiah 6, but he was out of excuses and he was ready to go.

You might be one of those leaders who appear to have always been comfortable with the idea of leadership, and who adapt to it easily and willingly. Perhaps you have found yourself drawn into leadership: I once heard someone describe his sense of call as a 'gentle awakening'. Or you may be a reluctant leader – reluctant perhaps because of an awareness of your limitations or because you feel overwhelmed by the task. Yet even though you have not gone looking for leadership, leadership has come looking for you.

In that case, you might find yourself easily identifying with at least some of what Moses expressed in his reluctance to accept his leadership assignment. Perhaps a fresh consideration of the Lord's promises will help strengthen you for the leadership that appears to be drawing you in, or in which you already find yourself.

But even though God listened to Moses' excuses and even appears to have made allowances for some of his fear by facilitating Aaron as a partner in the task, the whole incident is a reminder that God's calling on a leader's life is not accidental. Rather than being a casual invitation, it is a gracious summons.

Moses' adventure in leadership was ready to begin.

Questions for reflection

- How have you experienced a sense of calling in your life? Would you describe yourself as a reluctant leader, or have you found that you tend to gravitate easily to leadership roles?

- Which of Moses' excuses can you most identify with?
  - Who am I?
  - Who are You?
  - What about them?
  - What about this?
  - What about someone else?

4

Wise Leaders Know That Ministry is Best Shared

*I wish that all the LORD's people were prophets and that the
LORD would put his Spirit on them!*
(Numbers 11:29)

One of the reasons we do well to think of leadership as a collective process and not merely as an individual exercise arises from the fact that, by any reckoning, leadership involves responsibility, and at times, the responsibility is simply too much for one person to carry.

In this chapter we will be reflecting on two occasions when the story of Moses highlights the struggle he faced in attempting to shoulder the responsibility of leading the Israelites and when he was encouraged to share the load with others.

I can't help wondering if reluctant leaders (like Moses) might be more inclined to share leadership with others (at least in their more mature and sensible moments), given that it's not something they have grasped tightly for themselves. Could it be that some self-starters, especially those who have not yet fully realised that leadership is a gift from God, are more likely to struggle to hold their status with an open hand or share their role with others?

For all that many of the biblical examples of leadership are stories of charismatic or inspiring individuals, and for all that these examples may be deeply instructive, there is a danger, as Ian Parkinson has noted, that 'we can easily fall into the trap of conceiving leadership generally as a heroic activity that consists of the direct and directive actions of a prominent, solitary individual'.[58]

What if the heroic individual collapses under the load?

Moses and Jethro

By the time we get to chapter 18, Exodus has told us the story of the plagues, the first Passover and the crossing of the Red Sea, with the accompanying destruction of the Egyptian army. The text has also recorded the start of the people's food-related complaints and the provision of manna and quail. Chapter 17 continues the complaint theme at Massah and Meribah, and records Joshua's victory over Amalek.

In chapter 18 Moses was reunited with his family: as we have seen, his wife had previously gone back to her father, along with Moses' sons. On Jethro's arrival, Moses took the opportunity to fill him in on the remarkable events that had seen Pharaoh's power broken and the Lord rescue Israel. Jethro was impressed. He could see that the Lord,

---

[58] Parkinson, *Understanding Christian Leadership*, p63.

who had apparently appeared to his son-in-law and commissioned him for this remarkable enterprise, was greater than all other gods. He offered a sacrifice and joined Moses, Aaron and the elders of the people in a meal 'in the presence of God' (Exodus 18:12).

Had Jethro been converted? He was certainly close, and there is probably a good case to be made for such a reading of the story even if any claim that he had been won over to the exclusive worship of the Lord is not quite supported in the text.[59] Seeing the Lord as superior to all the other gods is not necessarily the same as submitting to the idea that there is no other god but Him.

You have probably heard people describe Jethro as the first management consultant in the Bible. However, as Arthur Boers reminds us, God's Spirit did not inspire Exodus 18 'to deliver a twenty-first-century leadership management lesson'.[60] This is a story about an outsider who responded positively to the Lord: Jethro is quite a contrast with Amalek, whose story is told in the previous chapter. It's also a story about grace from an unexpected source, as Moses, the man of God, received help from someone on the outside of the community.

It's certainly true that what Jethro saw the morning after the meal puzzled him and gave him significant cause for concern. The morning pattern appears to have been that Moses took a seat from which he would provide judgement on the various disputes that the people brought to him. It was a dawn to dusk affair: Moses sitting all day, with people standing around all day waiting for

[59] See Alexander, *Exodus*, p354.
[60] Boers, *Servants and Fools*, p30.

an appointment. If you thought that being put on hold while you wait to speak to someone in a call centre was bad, try this! And Moses' people were not even afforded the luxury of music to listen to while they waited!

Jethro first asked Moses to explain the rationale behind what was happening. The answer was that Moses was effectively functioning as the intermediary between God and the people when it came to understanding how life should be lived.

Jethro's concern was that Moses was likely to wear out both himself and the people. Why not focus on teaching and on the difficult cases, and delegate the rest of the work to others? These people would be carefully selected on the basis of their fear of God and their integrity, and the people would be organised into manageable-sized groups. Jethro's solution would be a win-win: Moses would be able to cope with the load, and the people would be a lot happier.

An outsider's perspective

During the difficult years of 'The Troubles' in Northern Ireland, I often thought that one of the challenges of resolving the conflict consisted in the fact that local people were too closely implicated in the issues behind what was happening to be able to agree a solution, while any outsider who might be better placed to come up with a 'neutral' solution would also struggle: for all of their objectivity, they would lack the sensitivity and instincts that could only come from being an insider.

But there can be value in an outsider's perspective, and one of the ways that Jethro's story might help us in thinking about leadership is that it demonstrates the value of such a perspective. Insiders and outsiders are likely to view a situation differently. While an outsider may fail to fully understand the inner workings or unspoken culture of an organisation (or a country) in the way an insider will grasp more easily, even instinctively, the outsider has a unique perspective which is easily missed by those who are so close to the situation that they can no longer see the forest for the trees.

For Moses and the people, what was happening on a day-by-day basis seems to have been accepted as just the way things were. One day was like the next. Why would it occur either to Moses or to the people that there might be another way to operate? What other way was there? This was simply how they did things. It took an observant outsider to point out the problem and propose a solution.

One of the guests on my podcast has been Russell Birney.[61] Russell served for several decades as a Presbyterian minister here in Northern Ireland. In our interview he told me about a conversation he had once with an outsider, himself a leader in another church context. He asked Russell to tell him about his typical programme. So he told him about Sundays. There was a Bible class at 10.00, a morning service at 11.30, then it was time for lunch at home before an afternoon service in a

---

[61] www.yourleadershipjourney.net/2019/01/15/the-leadership-journey-podcast-season-2-episode-15-russell-birney-part-2/ (accessed 2nd February 2021).

senior citizens' home which was followed by the evening service, and the youth fellowship.

Some of you who are leading in busy churches may be able to identify: it describes your Sunday.

His friend's response was a very blunt rejection of what was happening, and it began to dawn on Russell that this was no way to do ministry, or to be a leader. As with Moses, that realisation became part of a transition in his philosophy of ministry, and the adoption of a model of shared ministry.

That is the value of an outsider's view: if you've never done so before, maybe you should invite one to provide perspective on your church or organisation.

Even without the benefit of an outsider's perspective there is great value in leaders being able to extract themselves from the nitty-gritty of the day-to-day running of an organisation in order to be able to view their work from a different perspective, something that Moses had not been able to do by himself.

David Allen, pioneer of the *Getting Things Done* methodology, [62] uses a flying analogy to describe the varied perspectives from which work can be viewed. There is a difference between the view from the runway (what do you need to do now?) and the view from 50,000ft. A leader who always operates from 50,000ft is at risk, sooner or later, of losing touch with the detail of what is going on on the ground; but a leader who is always operating at ground level runs the risk of losing sight of the overall picture.

---

[62] David Allen, *Getting Things Done: How to Achieve Stress-free Productivity* (London: Piaktus, 2001).

During the time I pastored in Switzerland, my fellow-elders and I tried to make sure that we had an extended time every year in which we could reflect on some bigger-picture issues, or on the kinds of things that we would never have had time for in the midst of the week-by-week life of the church. Sometimes we would find a place to stay away overnight. There would be time for walks and time to enjoy meals together. There was time to pray and time to listen to God. I would say it is vital both for individuals and for leadership teams to carve out time like this: it may be very difficult, given the busyness of the organisational or ministry treadmill, but it's worth the effort. Constantly working in what Donald Schön called 'the swampy lowlands'[63] of practice and activity will certainly help to keep us earthed, but it may make it harder to gain a wider perspective.

The leader as bottleneck

To get back to Moses' *modus operandi*, the picture that Jethro observed is what it looks like when a leader becomes a bottleneck. When it happens, no one benefits. In Jethro's terms, both leader and people will wear themselves out (Exodus 18:18). The leader is overburdened and in danger of burnout, while the people who are forced to depend on the leader for every decision are also liable to be worn out waiting for them to give them a hearing and make a decision.

---

[63] Donald Schön used this expression in *The Reflective Practitioner* (New York: Basic Books, 1983).

There are several reasons why leaders fail to delegate. Some of them are organisational, where leaders have not developed the necessary skills to delegate well. What the leader considers as delegation might be more accurately described as abdication! Or, at the other end of the scale, perhaps the leader delegates but continues to micro-manage in a way that creates an oppressive atmosphere and leaves colleagues feeling cramped and undervalued.

However, there are also psychological reasons: for some reason the leader is unwilling to share responsibility. Perhaps they reckon that no one else will be able to do the job to their satisfaction, and the perfectionist in them cannot accept that. How often have you found yourself thinking that it would be quicker to do something yourself than to take the time to train someone who won't do it as well as you anyway? And, of course, if you delegate and someone makes a mess of a task, guess who has to clear it up?

On the other side of that particular coin, what if another person actually performs the task better than the leader? How can you justify your role if other people can do your job better than you?

Leaders who think like this have failed to grasp one of the counterintuitive aspects of power, namely that their power need not be diminished as they share it with others. In fact, it's a mark of maturity when a leader can give away power to others without fearing a loss of their own power or position. The second incident involving Moses and delegation will underline this point.

Before leaving the bottleneck episode, we should perhaps note that it is a little ironic that Moses should find himself in this position. After all, the previous chapter, with its account of the battle with Amalek, paints a picture of shared responsibility in that Moses delegates the military side of the operation to Joshua while he sets about the spiritual task of mediating God's power by holding out his staff. Even that responsibility had to be shared, with Aaron and Hur coming alongside to help hold his hands steady.

But it took the wise intervention of Jethro to help him extend this way of working beyond the battlefield.

Moses and the elders

Jumping ahead to Numbers 11, we find Moses overwhelmed with the responsibilities of leadership. Ruth Haley Barton comments that 'Moses was experiencing one of the paradoxes of leadership: that we can be surrounded by people and be very busy doing good things and yet feel deeply alone with the burdens we bear'.[64]

Moses was experiencing the loneliness of leadership responsibility.

The responsibility of leadership

Taking responsibility is an implicit part of leadership. Good leaders in any sphere are willing to be responsible, not only for the goals of their organisation, but also for the welfare of the people they lead. I have a colleague in my work at the Irish Bible Institute in Dublin who is a retired

---

[64] Barton, *Strengthening the Soul of Your Leadership*, p170.

Irish Army officer. When he talks about his years as a military officer, he reflects on how military leadership is more than simply giving orders to be obeyed: in his leadership he felt a real sense of responsibility for the well-being of those soldiers who had been entrusted to him.

Scripture makes it clear that spiritual leadership, not least leadership in the Church, is a responsibility tinged with sacred privilege.

One of the key passages providing an insight into Paul's view of Christian ministry is found in Acts 20. Pressed to be in Jerusalem by Pentecost, yet wanting to have the opportunity to speak with the church leaders from Ephesus, where he had previously spent time and had seen some very effective work take place, Paul sent for the Ephesian elders, asking them to meet him in Miletus, some thirty miles away.

His message to them outlines the responsibility of spiritual leadership, first through the illustration of his own example, and then through direct appeal. In his own ministry he had persevered through tears and trouble and been determined not to hold back from teaching anything that would benefit the Ephesian believers: he had taught them 'the whole will of God' (Acts 20:27). He appealed to the elders to 'keep watch' over themselves and over the flock the Holy Spirit had entrusted to their care (Acts 20:28).

The language of flocks and shepherds is familiar biblical language in discussions of leadership. As well as its use in the Old Testament, it's the language that Jesus (the Good Shepherd; see John 10) used with Peter as He recommissioned him by the shore of the Sea of Galilee

(John 21). Peter would later use that language in addressing the elders among the scattered recipients of his first letter (1 Peter 5:2).

Paul followed the same tradition when he told the Ephesian elders, in the episode referred to above, that they were to be 'shepherds of the church of God, which he bought with his own blood' (Acts 20:28).

This is the solemn privilege of church leadership. It is a gift, by appointment of the Holy Spirit, and it involves caring for something that has incalculable value to God.

Elsewhere in the New Testament the writer of Hebrews talks about the responsibility of leadership. Chapter 13 refers three times to leaders. Other than asking the Hebrews to 'greet' their leaders (v24), the writer says that they are to 'remember' those leaders who brought them the word of God (v7), and that they are to 'have confidence' in their current leaders, and 'submit to their authority' (v17).

In recent years, the term 'spiritual abuse' has made its way into discussions of Christian leadership. Any kind of authority can be misused or abused, and spiritual authority is no exception. Ecclesiological position and spiritual practice can be used in harmful ways.

Rather than read Hebrews 13 as giving leaders *carte blanche* to use their authority as they will, we need to pay attention to the reason the author gives for the injunction of verse 17: leaders have a solemn responsibility and they will be held accountable for the way in which they execute that responsibility. While the precise nature of that accountability is not specifically defined, it's best to understand it as an accountability to God, who has entrusted the responsibility to the leaders in the first place.

In his excellent book *Lead Like Joshua*, Derek Tidball writes about the need for leaders to take responsibility and notes that this will involve accountability. Reflecting on the ministry of the apostle Paul, he writes that:

> He was acutely conscious of his accountability to God for the quality of his work in the churches ... His eye was always on the day when he would present the results of his labour to God.[65]

Tidball suggests that the result of this was that his leadership 'was anything but coolly dispassionate, or indifferently professional, or clinically contractual'.[66] Instead, Paul gave himself to his task.

But the responsibility of spiritual leadership can weigh heavily on a leader, and that is what Moses had found by the time we get to Numbers 11.

Complaints about food had resurfaced (if they had ever really gone away), alongside more generalised complaints about the challenges of life on the move, so provoking the Lord to anger. Moses was 'troubled' (v10), and launched out on a strikingly frank complaint of his own, asking what he had done to displease the Lord for him to find himself in the midst of all this. They were not actually his children – he did not give birth to them – so why did he have to carry them around like a nurse carrying an infant?

---

[65] Derek Tidball, *Lead Like Joshua: Lessons for Today* (London: IVP, 2017), p4.
[66] Ibid, p5.

Where could he find food for them? He summed it all up with this:

> I cannot carry all these people by myself; the burden is too heavy for me. If this is how you are going to treat me, please go ahead and kill me right now – if I have found favour in your eyes – and do not let me face my own ruin.
> (Numbers 11:14-15)

Moses' desperation is echoed later in the Old Testament in the experience of Elijah. Queen Jezebel's threat, in the aftermath of the stunning events on Mount Carmel, was a powerful indicator that the hoped-for national revival was not guaranteed. Elijah may well have been in a state of both emotional and physical exhaustion (he certainly slept plenty in the next few days), and her threats were too much, so he ran. '"I have had enough, LORD," he said. "Take my life; I am no better than my ancestors"' (1 Kings 19:4).

Both of these remarkable servants of God reached a point where they were so overwhelmed that they could not envisage being able to continue either with their ministry or with life itself.[67]

In his book *Sustaining Leadership*, Paul Swann writes about his experience of 'fragility', describing a breakdown in his health that led to him having to step down from church leadership. As darkness descended and it felt that God had seemed to withdraw into the shadows, he

---

[67] Another prophet, Jonah, is on record as wanting his life to end (Jonah 4:8). Jonah's reasons were somewhat more selfish than those of either Moses or Elijah.

recounts how he identified with Elijah. 'It was not the thought of taking my own life that surfaced,' he writes, 'so much as the desire to not exist, to not have to bear life any longer as it had become.'[68]

Most leadership professions should probably carry some kind of health warning: the evidence suggests that this is certainly true of church leadership. Mark Miller-McLemore tells the story of a pastor who went to see an insurance agent (a church member) about arranging car insurance. The agent showed him a list of professions, ranked according to risk: clergy members featured in the second-highest risk group. They were in the same category as loggers and deep-sea welders: less at risk than crab fishermen, but more at risk than munitions' workers.[69]

In addition to dealing with the same life-stressors as everyone else, church leaders face burdens related to conflict, role ambiguity, stress that often spills across the porous borders between church life and family life, and the old chestnut of expectations, spoken and unspoken, external and internal. This is not to mention the cultural challenges of providing leadership at times of great change and upheaval.

Not that they are the only ones whose task is made more complex at times of upheaval. A global pandemic has reminded us of the perils of planning and long-range forecasting. What happens when the money for your business runs out? Or when your business is deemed to be

---

[68] Paul Swann, *Sustaining Leadership* (Abingdon: BRF, 2018), p23.

[69] Mark Miller-McLemore, 'Revaluing "Self-Care" as a Practice of Ministry', *Journal of Religious Leadership*, Volume 10, No 1, Spring 2011.

no longer necessary? How do you explain that to staff whose financial future depends on their job continuing to exist? How do you plan in any sphere when, to borrow from church consultant John Truscott, it's as though you are 'crossing a stream by stepping stones in a thick fog'?[70]

The spectre of burnout

At times the stresses and responsibilities of leadership become greater than the leader's resources and ability to handle them. Even if the leader never actually uses the language of absolute desperation that we find on the lips of Elijah and of Moses, the spectre of burnout appears on the horizon.

The concept of burnout is associated with the names of Hebert Freudenberger and Christina Maslach. It's often understood as comprising three elements:

- 'Emotional exhaustion' (work is draining);

- 'Depersonalisation' (negativity in relationships);

- 'Reduced personal accomplishment' (feeling inadequate).[71]

Leslie Francis, who has carried out significant work on the well-being of church leaders, discusses two separate scales of psychological health in ministry: the 'Scale of Emotional

---

[70] twitter.com/johnnvtruscott/status/1285447650289037312?s=20 (accessed 13th October, 2021). Used with permission.
[71] See Christina Maslach, *Burnout: The Cost of Caring* (Los Altos, CA: Malor Books, 2003).

Exhaustion in Ministry', which takes account of such themes as frustration and negativity, and the 'Satisfaction in Ministry Scale', which refers to such things as personal satisfaction and finding purpose in one's work.[72] Clearly, the combination of a high degree of exhaustion and a low sense of satisfaction can spell trouble.

Increasing attention has been paid in recent years to some of these challenges and to ways in which leaders can develop resilience. While some worry about the pendulum swinging too far in the direction of self-indulgence (and there is a danger that self-care can be a cover for selfishness or laziness as we forget the call to self-sacrifice), important work has been done on the theme of self-care – and rightly so. Just as the pre-flight briefing reminds air travellers to make sure their own oxygen mask is in place before attempting to help fellow-passengers with theirs, so Christian leaders are told to pay attention to themselves as well as to their ministry (Acts 20:28).

While there are clearly theological and doctrinal aspects to this (if a church leader begins to go adrift theologically, the drift will affect others), there are also devotional implications: it's sobering to read about Christian leaders who acknowledge that ministry has had a detrimental effect on their relationship with God. A burned-out leader, running on fumes, will struggle to lead

[72] Leslie J Francis, *Resilience and Wellbeing in Ministry: An empirical enquiry within the Church of Scotland*,
www.churchofscotland.org.uk/__data/assets/pdf_file/0008/56825/Resilience_and_Wellbeing_in_Ministry_-_full_report.pdf (accessed 12th November 2020). Used with permission.

well, and the collateral damage may be so great that we may not even need a Jethro to point it out.

Recently a friend shared with me a copy of a pre-ordination address by a former Archbishop of Canterbury, Donald Coggan. Part of his message focused on Acts 20 and Paul's warning to the Ephesian elders, and underlined the need for those in ministry to keep watch over themselves.

> The most tragic part of a bishop's life is that in which he has to deal with clergy who have *not* taken heed to themselves, when the bishop has perhaps to terminate a priest's ministry, or, almost equally tragically, to watch its formal continuance when the joy and power have gone from it, when prayer and sacrament and Bible study have died, and only the husk of the ministry remains. And all the time the bishop knows that this *could* happen to him.[73]

Sharing the load

So how did God respond to Moses' complaint?

Rather than end his leadership (or his life), He had a different solution: the responsibility of leadership would be shared (the people would also have more meat to eat than they would know what to do with).

Seventy of the elders were gathered. The Lord took some of the Spirit evident upon Moses and empowered

---

[73] Donald Coggan, *Convictions* (London: Hodder & Stoughton, 1975), p320.

the elders, who began to prophesy (apparently a one-off, see Numbers 11:25). Simply put, the answer to Moses' burden was for his leadership to be shared with others. For now at least, Moses would not have to carry the responsibility alone.

As is sometimes the case, however, the solution to one problem can lead to other problems. So it is that the narrative that follows the sharing of the Spirit goes on to touch on some of the challenges of shared leadership: what happens when you are no longer totally in control? Or, as Numbers 12 illustrates, what happens if plurality of leadership brings a set of relational issues such as jealousy and resentment?

Immediately after the sharing of the Spirit it emerged that there were two men – Eldad and Medad – who had not left the camp to gather with the others and with Moses. Yet they too were empowered by the Spirit, and as was the case with the others, they prophesied. Norman Cohen suggests that, like Miriam and Aaron (chapter 12), Eldad and Medad received their calling directly from God and not from Moses.[74]

How leaders respond when people start to operate outside their control is a test of wisdom. As I've already suggested in the discussion of the Exodus 18 incident, it's a mark of maturity when a leader can give away power to others without fearing a loss of their own power or position. Similarly, it's a sign of deepening wisdom when a leader is able to take genuine delight in the success or fruitfulness of someone else's ministry: others are viewed

---

[74] Cohen, *Moses and the Journey to Leadership*, p124.

not as rivals, but as co-workers, serving the same kingdom.

There is a striking contrast between the reactions of Moses and Joshua at the news of Eldad and Medad, and I think the contrast highlights something of the journey of maturity that a spiritual leader needs to navigate. Joshua, Moses' assistant and future successor, urged Moses to put a stop to these two men's prophetic ministry, but Moses wished that the prophetic gift could be extended to everyone (Numbers 11:28-29).

There has been speculation as to the content of Eldad and Medad's prophecy, including the suggestion that at least part of their message was that Moses would die and Joshua would lead the people into Canaan. However, the text itself doesn't elaborate, but instead draws attention to the theme of Joshua's jealousy.

The text also highlights the fact that Joshua had been Moses' assistant since his youth (v28): doubtless he had a keen sense of loyalty. Perhaps he felt that for two people from outside Moses' immediate sphere to have some kind of independent ministry seemed like a betrayal of his mentor: Moses really ought to tell them to stop.

Moses' response was to dismiss any need for Joshua to feel jealous on his account. This was not about Moses; it was about the welfare of the people of God: 'I wish that all the LORD's people were prophets and that the LORD would put his Spirit on them!' (v29).

Perhaps you have come across the statement that has sometimes been attributed to American president Harry Truman: 'It is amazing what you can accomplish if you do not care who gets the credit.' Even if the sentiment is inspiring, the attribution appears to be inaccurate: apparently a nineteenth-century Jesuit priest called Father Strickland may have been the first to express the idea when he wrote that 'a man may do an immense deal of good, if he does not care who gets the credit for it'.[75]

If that's true generally, how much more fruitful might our spiritual leadership be if we were free from the need to receive credit or to jealously guard our achievements as badges of honour that set us above others?

Ultimately, Moses' prayer was answered on the Day of Pentecost after Jesus' ascension when the Spirit was given, not to a few but to many, without distinction of age or gender: the work of ministry would no longer be the preserve of a select handful (Acts 2).

Moses' reaction to Joshua's concern challenges our understanding of leadership, and encourages us to move beyond any image of the heroic, solitary figure who either does everything by themselves or operates on a command-and-control basis. Wise leadership genuinely shares responsibility.

Fostering collaboration

Perhaps you have come across the claim made by an African proverb: 'If you want to go fast, go alone. If you

---

[75] For a discussion of the source of the quote, see www.quoteinvestigator.com/2010/12/21/doing-good-selfless/ (accessed 13th April 2021).

want to go far, go together.'[76] But what does it take to travel together and what are some of the qualities that need to be cultivated to make collaboration possible?

Whatever other qualities a leader needs in order to share the task of leadership, two in particular should be fairly close to the top of the list: humility and trust. Without these, the idea of shared leadership may never be much more than an aspiration. As we have already seen, Moses' concern was for the prosperity of the people of God and not for his own status as leader. Leadership that reverses those two things is headed for trouble.

Humility

Humility is orientated both vertically (in how we relate to God) and horizontally (in how we relate to other people). Vertically orientated humility takes seriously the idea that God is God and we are not. It recognises that we have nothing that has not been given to us. In God's presence it is more likely to say, 'God, have mercy on me, a sinner,' than, 'God, I thank you that I am not like other people.'[77] It accepts that 'God opposes the proud but shows favour to the humble' (1 Peter 5:5). A genuine vertically orientated humility can hardly help but overflow into its relationships with others.

---

[76] Note that there is some discussion about the exact origins of the proverb: see www.npr.org/sections/goatsandsoda/2016/07/30/487925796/it-takes-a-village-to-determine-the-origins-of-an-african-proverb?t=1618297301434 (accessed 13th April 2021).

[77] See Jesus' story about the two men at prayer in the temple (Luke 18:9-14).

Timothy Keller writes about what he calls 'gospel-humility', observing that 'the essence of gospel-humility is not thinking more of myself or thinking less of myself, it is thinking of myself less'.[78] In Keller's language, gospel-humility is 'the freedom of self-forgetfulness'.

It's several decades since Robert Greenleaf introduced the idea of 'servant leadership' into the vocabulary of leadership conversations.[79] For Greenleaf there is a difference between someone who is a leader first and who then chooses to serve, and someone who is servant first and whose choice to serve results in an aspiration to lead: *'the great leader is seen as servant first*, and that simple fact is the key to his greatness'.[80]

For obvious reasons, the concept of servant leadership resonates particularly with Christians who will want to point to the teaching and example of Jesus, which long predate the work of Robert Greenleaf. If anyone had a status that could be used to advantage, it was Jesus. Yet, as Paul writes in his Philippian letter, Jesus did not regard His status of equality with God as something to be held tightly for His own benefit: instead He chose the path of humility, and took on the form of a servant. His self-

[78] Timothy Keller, *The Freedom of Self-Forgetfulness: The Path to True Christian Joy* (Chorley: 10ofThose, 2012, Kindle Edition), loc.273.
[79] Those of us from more privileged backgrounds need to remember that the term 'servant' can carry negative connotations for people from different backgrounds, not least where slavery has been part of the history.
[80] Robert Greenleaf, *Servant Leadership: A Journey into the Nature of Legitimate Power and Greatness* (New York: Paulist Press, 1977, 2002), p21 (italics original).

humbling meant obedience 'to the point of death' (Philippians 2:6-8, ESV).

In His teaching, Jesus upended His disciples' understanding of greatness. The truly great people are not those with all the badges and trappings of power, but those who serve. In the hours before His crucifixion, He demonstrated His love for His disciples by washing their feet, thus setting the example of humble service that He intended to be characteristic of His followers, including those who would eventually become leaders.

Humble leaders will concern themselves with the welfare of those who are entrusted to their care: this will mean far more to them than their own position or reputation. As Paul Tripp writes, 'you love serving more than you crave leading'.[81]

In terms of collaboration, humility means recognising one's own limitations: it's a wise leader who manages to do this before either circumstances or the observations of others force them to admit them. It also means accepting and genuinely valuing the contributions of others. The wisdom of humility refuses to view others as threats to one's own status, or to see them merely as a means to getting something done.

Trust

If humility allows me to recognise my limitations and accept and value the contributions of others, trust is what allows collaborative relationships to function and flourish.

---

[81] Paul David Tripp, *Lead: 12 Principles for Leadership in the Church* (Wheaton, IL: Crossway, 2020), p24.

Trust is a core component of leadership as it is the vital currency of human relationships. Not only do people need to be able to have confidence in their leaders, but leaders must also cultivate an ability to trust their followers: failure to do so is likely to result in an oppressive, perhaps dictatorial, system of governance. Leaders must also trust each other if the tasks and responsibilities of leadership are to be properly shared.

Patrick Lencioni's *The Five Dysfunctions of a Team* is a brilliant exposition of what happens to a team when there is a lack of trust. He uses a leadership fable to describe the five dysfunctions of the book's title, which he sets out in the form of a pyramid. At the base of the pyramid, thus foundational to the other four dysfunctions, is 'an absence of trust'. He writes, 'Trust lies at the heart of a functioning, cohesive team. Without it, teamwork is all but impossible.'[82]

For Lencioni, the absence of trust goes hand in hand with an unwillingness to be vulnerable. It goes much further than trusting a colleague to follow a particular course of action: it's the ability of team members to trust one another with their weaknesses and vulnerabilities. Trust in this sense allows a team member to admit limitations and ask for help. It means being able to be questioned about their role. It means appreciating the expertise of others. It means giving one another the benefit of the doubt, and being able to apologise.

---

[82] Patrick Lencioni, *The Five Dysfunctions of a Team: A Leadership Fable* (San Francisco, CA: Jossey-Bass, 2002), p195.

Wise leaders, who recognise the value of shared leadership and wish to involve others in their work, will be keen to cultivate humility and trust.

What if I am the solo leader?

Leaders who enjoy the privilege of being part of a team of like-minded people (hopefully not simply clones) need to realise the privilege they have. Some leaders, at least for a season, find themselves in lonely and isolated circumstances: the prospect of seven people, never mind seventy, to share the load is a faraway pipe dream.

Consider the minister of a small, ageing congregation who carries sole responsibility for pastoring, preaching, praying and photocopying. Or the pioneering leader of a small charity, struggling with the limited resources available from what is no more than a small group of volunteers. Not only do people in such circumstances have to cope with the challenge of carrying responsibility, but the weight of this may be compounded by loneliness, a not unusual side effect of leadership.

Each individual's circumstances and personality are different from someone else's, so there is no one-size-fits-all solution to these issues.

As well as being a challenge – often deeply painful – for individual leaders, it's a challenge for those charged with caring for these leaders in the context of organisational or denominational structures.

Perhaps, too, it's time for a few more Jethros who are willing to come alongside leaders – not least those isolated leaders who are struggling under the weight of their responsibility – and communicate affirmation and wise encouragement.

Jethro was a gift in the desert. But Moses needed more. Without the evident presence of God with him, what was the point of the whole exercise?

Questions for reflection

- Do you find it difficult to share responsibility with others? Why?

- Do you ever seek out the perspective of an 'outsider' in order to seek ways of increasing your leadership effectiveness?

- The chapter highlighted the importance of humility and trust in relation to collaboration: are there other qualities you would add?

5
Wise Leaders Know That God Loves Them

You have found favour in my sight, and I know you by name.
(Exodus 33:17, ESV)

I have a little piece of calligraphy on a card in my Bible. It features these words, adapted from Henri Nouwen: 'Listen to the voice that calls you the Beloved.'[83]

Nouwen's language is drawn from words spoken at the start of Jesus' ministry when Jesus had just been baptised by John the Baptist (a somewhat confused John, who thought Jesus should be baptising him, not vice versa). It was the Father who spoke these words of acceptance and affirmation: 'You are my Son, whom I love; with you I am well pleased' (Mark 1:11).

I must admit to a degree of ambivalence about Nouwen's application of the language. After all, there is a

---

[83] See Henri Nouwen, *You are the Beloved: Daily Meditations for Spiritual Living* (London: Hodder & Stoughton, 2017), p164.

uniqueness to Jesus' sonship: none of the rest of us can lay claim to God's fatherhood in exactly the same way as Jesus. If we get that wrong, we're into all kinds of Trinitarian confusion!

That said, I think all of us – leaders or not – have a deep longing to hear words like these. Part of the reason that's not always straightforward is that, as Nouwen suggests, there are various voices trying to gain our attention.[84] Perhaps you can think of some that seem more vivid to you than the message of the Father's love. It can be hard to silence the nagging voices that tell us we are desperate failures or hypocrites, that we will never amount to much, that we are wasting our time, or that at best God tolerates us but probably doesn't like us, and if He actually loves us, it's not with any great degree of affection.

With all that going on, how precious it would be to think that there is a voice that tells us we are loved.

One of the things that has most struck me in the past few years as I have talked with various Christian leaders, initially in the context of my doctoral work and more recently in my *Leadership Journey* series of podcasts, has been the recurring theme of God's love.

Phil Emerson leads an active and thriving church in Lurgan, Northern Ireland. He started the church more than twenty years ago in his living room, out of a desire to see a church that would care for the kinds of families he was meeting in the course of a job delivering coal: families

[84] Henri Nouwen, *The Still, Small Voice of Love*,
www.henrinouwen.org/meditation/the-still-small-voice-of-love/
(accessed 13th November 2020).

in some of whose homes people were having to choose between furniture and fuel.

When Phil was a guest on my podcast,[85] he talked about an experience he had had some twenty-five years previously when he'd been working as a lorry driver. Early one morning he found himself standing on top of an industrial tank when he had such a dramatic encounter with God that he 'nearly fell off the top of the tank'.

> I was thirty-three, and I realised for the first time in my life that God loved me … I had a baptism of God's love. I always thought that God was just like the angry father who tolerated me, and loved me but didn't really like me, and sort of put up with me.
> Something happened, and it was like a baptism of the love of God, and it broke me and I wept and wept and wept, and it went on for days.

It was not that Phil was not a Christian or that he had no understanding of the gospel. In our conversation he recounted that he had come to personal faith as a young child. But this experience was utterly life-changing for him: as he put it, he 'saw God through a different lens'.

To some of you, that probably sounds like raw emotionalism, and emotionalism makes you wary. Other readers will happily see the incident as a gracious intervention of God in Phil's life.

---

[85] www.yourleadershipjourney.net/2018/09/25/the-leadership-journey-podcast-season-two-episode-two-philip-emerson-part-2/ (accessed 3rd February 2021).

For what it's worth, I've noticed that Phil's experience is not completely unique.

To take another example, Malcolm Duncan is a well-known pastor and leader in the UK. Like Phil Emerson, he has been a guest on my podcast and, like Phil, he also shared an account of a powerful emotional experience around the theme of the love of God.

He was in his early twenties and had taken a youth group to a Christian concert in Motherwell, Scotland. The performer was the legendary Larry Norman. At one point he stopped, looked out into the audience and, as Malcolm recalls it, spoke these words:

> There's nothing that you can do that'll make God love you any more, and there's nothing that you can do that will make God love you any less. And you'll never disillusion Him because He never had any illusions about you in the first place!

Here's how Malcolm described what happened to him:

> All I know is that God broke my heart and I started to cry. So much so that I couldn't drive the minibus back to where I was staying.
> And for three weeks I got up every day and cried all day, drank water only, and went to bed that night.

> God … was reaching into my soul … and He was pulling out the hurt and the heartbreak … and slowly He was replacing it with something else.[86]

What happened had a profoundly transforming effect. Previously, Malcolm confessed to a rock-bottom self-image: he believed himself to be worthless. After this experience he knew that he had value and purpose.

Stories like these – and they are not the only ones I have listened to – make me think that there are times when God goes out of His way to provide a special assurance of His love to some of those whom He calls as leaders.

I'm well aware that some of you may be a little nervous at this point: you are concerned that I am advocating some form of uncontrolled subjectivity. Indeed! I agree that we need to be cautious about making uncontrolled subjective experience the sole validation of spiritual truth. Nonetheless, I think there is also a danger in being so committed to a left-brained pursuit of absolute objectivity (as if that was something we could ever reach), that the emotional side of our spirituality ends up in a state of stunted atrophy. We have been created with both minds and emotions, and we will be lopsided as long as we pursue one to the point where we deny the other.

Too many of us have grown accustomed to the idea of God as an austere, somewhat distant figure, and we have allowed this picture to hide the picture of a God who rejoices over His people 'with singing' (Zephaniah 3:17). He is the Father who runs to us in Christ like the prodigal

---

[86] www.yourleadershipjourney.net/2018/06/19/the-leadership-journey-podcast-28-malcolm-duncan-part-three/ (accessed 2nd February 2021).

father of Luke 15 whose joy over his son ensured that the boy's shame was covered and his status was restored. Wouldn't you love to have seen that joyful father running along a dusty road to reach his bedraggled and disgraced son as quickly as he possibly could, to throw his arms around him and embrace him with kisses of compassion and acceptance? Some of us, who doubt the depth of God's affection for us, might need to adjust our functional theology to accommodate a picture of a God like that.

More than theoretical

Though he would never seek to minimise clarity of doctrine, Paul wanted those in his care to have more than a theoretical understanding of the love of God. In his second major prayer in his Ephesian letter, he prayed that the believers (this was not just something for leaders) would be able 'to grasp how wide and long and high and deep is the love of Christ, and to know this love that surpasses knowledge' (Ephesians 3:18-19). As F F Bruce observed in his commentary, this 'cannot be other than an experimental knowledge'.[87] Similarly, Romans 5 talks about the love of God that is demonstrated in the cross (objective truth) and 'poured out into our hearts through the Holy Spirit' (verse 5, subjective experience). It is the work of the Spirit to open our hearts to the experience of God's love.

---

[87] F F Bruce, *The Epistles to the Colossians, to Philemon and to the Ephesians,* The New International Commentary on the New Testament (Grand Rapids, MI: Eerdmans, 1984), p329.

In his recent book on the heart of Christ, Dane Ortlund writes this:

> It is one thing, as a child, to be told your father loves you. You believe him. You take him at his word. But it is another thing, unutterably more real, to be swept up in his embrace, to feel the warmth, to hear his beating heart within his chest, to instantly know the protective grip of his arms. It's one thing to hear he loves you; it's another thing to feel his love. This is the glorious work of the Spirit.[88]

Moses and the favour of God

In Exodus 33 Moses faced a major dilemma: what would happen if God Himself were not to travel with the people to the land of promise? At the start of the chapter, God said that He would send an angel with them, but He Himself would not go: the stubborn, rebellious streak in the Israelites' character would put them at risk of His judgement.

Moses enjoyed a remarkable relationship with God. For one thing, there was an earthy authenticity to the relationship, as we've seen in his attempts to dodge God's call on the edge of the Midianite desert. There was a searing honesty, as seen in his cry for help when he was faced with the overwhelming challenge of responsibility for the welfare of so many people.

---

[88] Dane Ortlund, *Gentle and Lowly: The Heart of Christ for Sinners and Sufferers* (Wheaton, IL: Crossway, 2020), p122.

The text of Exodus 33 takes us to the heart of the relationship, with the mind-stretching observation, 'The LORD would speak to Moses face to face, as one speaks to a friend' (Exodus 33:11). Later, the Lord would contrast how he spoke to prophets in visions and dreams with how he spoke to Moses 'face to face, clearly and not in riddles' (Numbers 12:8).

The news that God would not go with them was not something that Moses was about to accept without a debate. Why should these people go anywhere if God would not be with them? It was God's presence with them that would distinguish them from any other people. After all, God had promised to dwell among them: that was why He had redeemed them (Exodus 29:46).

In some ways, the story of the Bible is the story of God living among His people. To begin with, He walked in the Garden of Eden. Following the Exodus, His presence was mediated through the tabernacle – a mobile sanctuary – and then in the temple. Things changed with the dawning of the New Testament and the coming of Jesus: He is the Word made flesh who 'lived in his tent'[89] among men and women (John 1:14), before sending His Spirit to indwell the Church, not only as a people, but also as individuals. The promise of the new heaven and new earth is that God's dwelling place will once more be 'among the people, and he will dwell with them' (Revelation 21:3).

The twenty-first century Church should aspire to be known for the living and perceptible presence of God. For sure there will be elements of belief and behaviour that mark out the Church as clearly different from other

---

[89] D A Carson, *The Gospel according to John* (Leicester: IVP, 1991), p127.

groups, but we are to be distinguished by the special presence of an omnipresent God.

The Lord listened to Moses' concern:

> And the LORD said to Moses, 'I will do the very thing you have asked, because I am pleased with you and I know you by name.'
> (Exodus 33:17)

Or, as the ESV has it, 'you have found favour in my sight'.

You can almost hear the echoes of the Father's words at the baptism of Jesus. Moses had found the grace and favour of God, a God who knew him by name. Of all the incredible things that Moses experienced in the course of his leadership journey, how precious to enjoy such a relationship with God.

'Listen to the voice that calls you the Beloved.'

Names written in heaven

Around the middle of Luke's Gospel account, Jesus sends out seventy-two[90] disciples on mission. They are to go ahead of Jesus to places where He will soon visit. When they get back their mood is buoyant. The mission has been spectacular, as demons have submitted to them in the name of Jesus. However, Jesus makes it clear to them that no matter what spiritual authority they have been given, there is a deeper source of joy. He tells them, 'However, do not rejoice that the spirits submit to you, but rejoice that your names are written in heaven' (Luke 10:20).

---

[90]There is textual variation, with some manuscripts stating 'seventy'.

There is an important leadership principle in this statement. For most of us, the story of our leadership will be a story that mixes highs and lows. Perhaps the highs include a successful new initiative that expanded your organisation or your ministry's sphere of influence. Perhaps it's the growth of your church, a season of many conversions, or a particularly meaningful preaching series that seems to have led to tangible change in the life of the congregation.

Do not rejoice in the number of converts, or the growth of your sphere of influence: rejoice that your name is written in heaven!

If our joy is tied only to our success stories, what happens when we fail? What happens when you watch someone you've mentored cut loose from their spiritual moorings? What happens when half a dozen families leave the church? What happens when economic conditions outside your control mean that you need to reduce your organisation's operations and embark on a series of redundancies? What happens to your joy then?

But if your most fundamental source of joy is to be known and accepted by God, then even as you grieve your leadership disappointments, you can still rejoice that your name is written in heaven.

The value of solitude

There is a section in Luke 6 where Jesus prayed through the night, called His disciples in the morning and then went on to minister to the crowds. In his reflection on this, Henri Nouwen suggests that the night was for solitude, the morning for community and the afternoon for ministry. The sequence is important. In a culture of activism, we may be tempted to get straight into mission and ministry, but this sequence 'begins by being with God in solitude; then it creates a fellowship, a community of people with whom the mission is being lived; and finally this community goes out together to heal and to proclaim good news'.[91]

But what is the purpose of solitude, the starting point?

Solitude, says Nouwen, is 'the place [where we] can listen to the voice of the One who calls [us] the beloved'.

Here is why Nouwen says it matters that we grasp this assurance:

> If you keep that in mind, you can deal with an enormous amount of success as well as an enormous amount of failure without losing your identity, because your identity is that you are the beloved. Long before your father and mother, your brothers and sisters, your teachers, your church, or any people touched you in a loving as well as in a wounding way – long before you were rejected by some person or praised by somebody else – that voice has been there always. 'I have loved you with an everlasting love.'[92]

---

[91] Henri Nouwen, 'From Solitude to Community to Ministry', *Leadership*, 16:2, Spring 1995, p81.
[92] Ibid, p82.

The challenges of maintaining a devotional life

That Moses enjoyed a face-to-face, friend-to-friend relationship with God should inspire us, especially once we see how significant hearing God's voice is for our stability and the health of our leadership. While Moses' calling and role were unique, Scripture invites us in our turn to draw near. The Irish hymn writer Joseph Scriven, who grew up not far from where I am writing these words, grasped something of the idea of prayer's friendship when he wrote his famous hymn:

> What a friend we have in Jesus,
> all our sins and griefs to bear!
> What a privilege to carry
> everything to God in prayer!
> O what peace we often forfeit,
> O what needless pain we bear,
> all because we do not carry
> everything to God in prayer![93]

What a fantastic encouragement to prayer! Yet the path to this sacred friendship is not without its hindrances.

So much to do

For one thing, there is a lot to do. This means that various things jostle for our attention. It can be tempting to prioritise what can be measured (how many hours we

---

[93] Joseph Medlicott Scriven (1819-86), 'What a Friend We Have in Jesus' (Public Domain, 1855).

worked, how many people we counselled, how many articles we wrote, how many emails we sent); but what if the things that most deeply matter cannot actually be measured? An hour working through tasks on today's list appears more productive than an hour of solitude and silence with an open Bible. Which will we choose?

We have all heard people talk about being a Mary in a Martha world. We sometimes read Luke's story of the two sisters in a way that has Martha representing the activists, working their way through an ever-increasing to-do list, while Mary is the reflective who is more interested in being still than being busy (Luke 10:38-42).

The obvious problem with oversimplifying the story is that if we were all Marys, there would be no one to cook dinner. Beyond that, I don't think we should isolate the story from the rest of the Bible in a way that makes it read like a snub to service. After all, the same chapter that gives us the story of Mary and Martha records Jesus' telling of the story of the Good Samaritan with its 'go and do likewise' application (v37), as well as recounting the story of the seventy-two missionaries we mentioned earlier. Jesus Himself dignified the tasks of service.

But the story is a reminder that there are times when we can get so weighed down by the list of what needs to be done (or what we think needs to be done) that we serve from resentment rather than from the overflow of devoted hearts. There is at least a hint in the text that Martha's issue arose from wanting to overcomplicate the meal she was preparing for Jesus and His friends. Jesus spoke to her about how she was 'upset about many things' (v41). Could it be that instead of a simple dish of lentils and fish, which would have been quite enough, Martha was keen to offer several types of fish, a couple of chicken dishes and a selection of bread to go with the lentils? Perhaps there would even be a choice of Pavlova or apple crumble for dessert. Is that why Jesus said that only one thing was needed? Keep it simple, Martha!

The problem was that an overburdened Martha had grown resentful of Mary. Her stress over what she thought needed to be done had led her to devalue what Mary was doing.

Isn't it sobering to think that work we do *for* God can lead to us neglecting and devaluing time we simply spend *with* God?

Easily distracted?

Then there is the issue of distraction. Blaise Pascal, the seventeenth-century French philosopher, famous for his triangle and his wager, wrote about his discovery that 'all the unhappiness of men arises from one single fact, that they cannot stay quietly in their own chamber'.[94] More recently, and in similar vein, Richard Foster has said that 'distraction is the primary spiritual problem in our day'.[95]

Aside from our preoccupation with the mountain of tasks that are calling for our attention, there are our own inner thoughts – our preoccupations, fears, confusion and questions. This is not even to mention the ubiquitous

---

[94] Blaise Pascal, *Pensées* (Mineola, NY: Dover Publications, 2018), p39.
[95] Richard Foster, *Sanctuary of the Soul: Journey into Meditative Prayer* (London: Hodder & Stoughton, 2011), p104.

distractions – and addictions – of our social media feeds or the on-demand news cycles.

Henri Nouwen describes our struggle with distraction with this vivid picture:

> The trouble is, as soon as you sit and become quiet, you think, *Oh, I forgot this. I should call my friend. Later on I'm going to see him.* Your inner life is like a banana tree filled with monkeys jumping up and down.[96]

Scripture invites us, 'Be still, and know that I am God' (Psalm 46:10). We need to identify the sources of our distraction, be they the restless internal voices of guilt or anxiety or the external stimuli of endless news feeds or social media notifications, and learn to cultivate this stillness in our hearts.

The ministry substitute

A third, subtle issue – particularly for those in church leadership or other vocational ministry – is that ministry can become a substitute for devotion, which leads to our becoming 'professional Christians'. Perhaps we naively imagine that now that we are 'in ministry' we have graduated beyond the normal routines of the Christian life. Or it's simply that our reading and study of the Bible for sermons and talks that we will deliver for others somehow takes the place of reading it for ourselves, for the nourishment of our own souls.

---

[96] Nouwen, 'From Solitude to Community to Ministry', p83.

Ruts and routines

Then there are the issues around routine. Some of us grew up with the 'quiet time', the practice of setting aside some time for Bible reading – often with the help of Bible-reading notes – and personal prayer. It's a valuable routine, but any routine can become a rut, and we also need to realise that something that works well for a particular personality or temperament may need adjustment for someone else.

While some may be tempted to dismiss spiritual routine as the enemy of spontaneity, or even a pathway to legalism, we need to realise that without routine or structure we are at the mercy of our moods and circumstances. Routines, as long as we work to keep them fresh, help us not to lose sight of what is important. Remember, too, not to confuse the goal and the means: the goal of your 'quiet time' should not be to see how much of the Bible you can read in a year, it's to allow your heart to connect with God.

Jesus loves me, this I know

The simple truth of the love of Jesus can be accessible to a small child and yet remain precious to a seasoned leader. If I may adapt Gregory the Great's statement about Scripture:[97] God's love is like a river – it is shallow enough

---

[97] 'It is, as it were, a kind of river, if I may so liken it, which is both shallow and deep, wherein both the Lamb may find a footing, and the elephant float at large.' S Gregory the Great, *Morals on the Book of Job*:

for a lamb to wade in, but deep enough for an elephant to swim.

Yet I wonder how many of us have grown up singing the words of 'Jesus Loves Me',[98] that well-loved children's hymn, but have allowed their purity and simplicity to lose their grip on our hearts. It can take a while for a deep assurance of that love to sink into our subjective experience.

This is a great challenge for any leader. The demands of leadership and its ever-increasing complexities could easily drive all of us to distraction. Add to the mix those negative voices that tell us that we are unlikely ever to amount to much (so we'd better try even harder to prove them wrong) or that our time would be better invested in something other than what we have felt called to do (again, try harder to prove the voice wrong, or just give up): soon the 'gentle whisper' (1 Kings 19:12) of the Father is drowned out.

Philip Yancey tells the story of having to spend several hours in an airport, waiting for a flight to take him to a conference where he was to speak. He spent the time talking to a woman who was on her way to the same conference. The tone of their conversation was fairly downbeat, perhaps not surprising since it was late and the flight had been delayed for five hours. They talked about their disappointments with church and their questions of faith. At the time Yancey was writing his book

---

A Library of Fathers of the Holy Catholic Church, Vol 1, Parts 1 & 2 (Oxford: John Henry Parker, 1844), p9.

[98] Anna Bartlett Warner (1827-1915), 'Jesus Loves Me' (Public Domain, 1859).

Disappointment with God and felt burdened by the doubts and unanswered prayers of others.

Here is how Yancey recounts what happened:

> My companion listened to me in silence for a very long time, and then out of nowhere she asked a question that has always stayed with me. 'Philip, do you ever just let God love you?' she said. 'It's pretty important, I think.'
> I realized with a start that she had brought to light a gaping hole in my life. For all my absorption in the Christian faith, I had missed the most important message of all. The story of Jesus is the story of a celebration, a story of love.[99]

John Greenleaf Whittier expressed it beautifully in part of his hymn 'Dear Lord and Father of Mankind'.

> Drop Thy still dews of quietness,
> Till all our strivings cease;
> Take from our souls the strain and stress,
> And let our ordered lives confess
> The beauty of Thy peace.
>
> Breathe through the heats of our desire
> Thy coolness and Thy balm;
> Let sense be dumb, let flesh retire;

---

[99] Philip Yancey, *The Jesus I Never Knew* (Grand Rapids, MI: Zondervan, 1995), p269.

Speak through the earthquake, wind, and fire,
O still, small voice of calm![100]

'Listen to the voice that calls you the Beloved.'

Questions for reflection

- How much of a priority is it for you to cultivate a relationship with God that brings subjective assurance rather than simply adding to your stocks of intellectual knowledge about Him?

- Which of the barriers discussed in the chapter (overload, distraction, professionalism, routine) do you encounter most in your devotional life?

- 'Do you ever just let God love you?'

[100] John Greenleaf Whittier (1807-1892), 'Dear Lord and Father of Mankind' (Public Domain, 1872).

6
Wise Leaders Know That They Cannot Escape Criticism

Now Moses was a very humble man, more humble than anyone
else on the face of the earth.
(Numbers 12:3)

In the middle of the eighteenth century, Benjamin Franklin developed the use of lightning rods – pointed pieces of metal, placed on the top of buildings, whose purpose was to protect those buildings from damage during lightning strikes. I'll leave it to my scientific friends to explain the details of how the system works, but figuratively, the term has come to describe someone who takes blame or criticism, even though they are not totally responsible for a particular situation. While it may not be formally listed as part of your job description, if you have been in leadership for any length of time, you have probably discovered that being a lightning rod comes with the territory!

I don't know who first put it like this, but it's a sobering thought that if God calls you to be a leader, you give up the right to always be understood. Unless a leader chooses to be little more than a caretaker whose main priority consists in attempting to keep everyone happy, they can expect conflict and criticism. I suspect that the leader who has never been criticised has probably never attempted to achieve much through their leadership; mind you, I suspect that even that is unlikely to keep critics at bay, as they will be criticised for inertia. Reggie McNeal says that 'the decision to serve as a spiritual leader signs one up for conflict',[101] something that appears to escape the notice of many aspiring leaders until they discover that those they are serving refuse their leadership and turn against them.

It needs to be said that not all conflict and criticism are bad. If they are approached in the right way and for the right reasons, conflict and criticism can be constructive and helpful. Some of us struggle to accept that. They don't seem to be very 'Christian' concepts. After all, Jesus told us that we were to turn the other cheek and go the extra mile (Matthew 5:38-42). He lauded the peacemakers (Matthew 5:9). Paul wrote that we are to do what we can to 'live at peace with everyone' (Romans 12:18). As Ian Parkinson observes, 'there are a good number of people who assume that any level of disagreement between people must inevitably be destructive and wrong, and should thus be guarded against at all costs'.[102]

However, peace-making is not the same thing as peace-faking, and the avoidance of conflict is not always noble.

[101] McNeal, *A Work of Heart*, loc.2296.
[102] Parkinson, *Understanding Christian Leadership*, p208.

Leaders who cannot distinguish between different kinds of criticism or conflict are likely to become unhelpfully defensive and deny themselves potential avenues of growth. This can be a particular challenge for people involved in vocational church ministry, where it can be painfully difficult to fully separate a person's identity from their work.

Take preachers, whose role lays them open to the weekly evaluation of dozens or hundreds of listeners, some of whom are not short of a strong opinion or two. After all, these listeners can compare their preacher to any number of polished communicators with a flashy podcast. So when someone, out of genuine concern for your development, offers the suggestion that your preaching would be more effective if you shaved eight minutes off your typical forty-minute effort, or if you worked a bit longer at developing the element of application in your sermons, what the insecure preacher thinks they're hearing is that it's time to seek a new calling.

Of course, one of the particular issues for pastors and ministers is that the same tender-heartedness that equips them to be sensitive to the pastoral needs of their flock leaves them vulnerable to having their own hearts wounded. It's not always easy to cultivate a tough skin and a tender heart at the same time. Perhaps it's the wounds that have been inflicted during moments of unkind, excessively personal criticism that have contributed to some leaders' defensiveness, and that has made them overly vulnerable to the slightest critique.

Whatever its roots, the defensiveness of a fragile ego that is unable or unwilling to trust the good intentions of others can be relationally harmful in addition to limiting the leader's personal development.

In Chapter Four, I referred to Patrick Lencioni's book, *The Five Dysfunctions of a Team*, noting the importance he attaches to the need for trust between team members. A lack of trust is at the base of team dysfunction. It is because team members fail to trust each other, refusing to make themselves vulnerable, that they attempt to avoid conflict. Substantive issues are not properly discussed because there is insufficient trust to sustain rigorous debate and difference of opinion.

Nonetheless, whatever the value of constructive conflict – and leaders need to learn to welcome it and use it, whether it is to hone vision or improve an organisation's effectiveness, or whether it is to correct a personal blind spot – there remains a destructively critical kind of conflict that can easily sap a leader's energy and cause great pain.

Much of what Moses faced in terms of the challenges of leadership came in the form of such conflict.

A taste of things to come

If he thought about it during his leadership years, perhaps a preview of what lay ahead had come forty years earlier, on the day when Moses attempted to separate two quarrelling Hebrews (Exodus 2:13-14): remember that on the previous day he had killed an Egyptian who had been mistreating a Hebrew.

In his speech to the Sanhedrin, Stephen makes this comment on the episode: 'Moses thought that his own people would realise that God was using him to rescue them, but they did not' (Acts 7:25).

Perhaps it was not an entirely unreasonable assumption on Moses' part. After all these years of servitude and mistreatment, here at last was someone who would fight their corner. Surely the stage was set and the time was right for Moses to step up.

But it was not to be: at least, not yet.

While the text of Exodus does not elaborate on what happened next with the two quarrelling Hebrews (did they resume their fight?), it would have been ironic if Moses' intervention had caused them to forget their own quarrel in order to focus on the interfering outsider. At least Moses' intervention would have had the value of leading unwittingly to some kind of reconciliation!

How many new leaders have ridden into town, convinced that they are God's answer to every question, His solution to every problem, only to find that the people they have come to serve are not convinced? Worse, as they begin to involve themselves in some of the issues that need sorting, they discover that old hostilities are redirected and they become the target.

Stephen goes on to note how Moses was pushed aside with the words, 'Who made you ruler and judge over us?' (Acts 7:27). Any sense that he might have assumed of being on a mission was instantly called into question. When he realised that his act of the previous day had not remained secret, and that the Hebrews would not provide him with a safe place, he took flight.

In time, of course, Moses would return and would serve as judge and ruler over Israel, but during his leadership years there would be clear echoes of this early rejection.

How do you lead people who don't want to accept your leadership? I suspect that, for many, that is more than a merely theoretical question. Any answer needs to be as multifaceted as the reasons for the leader's rejection. Sometimes reluctant followers may have good reason for their reluctance, and at times it may be the leader, rather than the followers, who needs to be encouraged to step off the bus, or at least examine their attitude. But there may be times when a leader has been above reproach and may have done everything possible to lead well, but they still face the rejection and hostility of those who will not accept their leadership.

Moses' first attempt to lead the Hebrews was derailed. His time to lead would come, but not before he spent those forty years in exile that we considered earlier. Even then, and God's clear call notwithstanding, he would still face opposition and challenges to his leadership. The path of leadership can be long and painful.

Bricks without straw

There is a second taster of things to come. Forty years had passed. They were years of obscurity for Moses and years of pain and groaning for the Hebrew slaves. And as we have seen, Moses had finally had to get over his excuses and accept God's call to leadership.

When Moses and Aaron gathered the Israelite elders together to report on Moses' encounter with God, the initial response was positive. The people heard that God was on the move. Moses' signs fed their faith, and they believed. Their suffering had not escaped God's attention or His concern, and so they worshipped.

However, the positivity was short-lived. God had warned Moses that Pharaoh would not give up his labour force without a struggle (Exodus 4:21), and sure enough, Moses' and Aaron's initial request was met with a pretty sharp response: 'Who is the LORD, that I should obey him and let Israel go? I do not know the LORD and I will not let Israel go' (Exodus 5:2).

As far as Pharaoh was concerned, Moses and Aaron were simply interrupting the people's work. If they had time to be thinking about heading off for a few days to worship God, they clearly did not have enough to do. Their work would have to be made more demanding: let them make bricks without straw.

It's hard not to notice some parallels with the busy drivenness that seems to mark so much of life in the contemporary Western world.

It remains to be seen exactly what impact Covid-19 will have on patterns of work – for example, how many people will make the transition to working from home, at least part of the time, thus cutting out significant amounts of time spent commuting – but in recent decades being busy has become a badge of honour. If you are not busy, you are almost afraid to admit it, in case people think there must be something wrong with you.

Although it's a little dated by now, in 2008 Professor Michael Zigarelli published the results of an extensive survey that aimed to explore obstacles to growth among Christians. Some 20,000 Christians were surveyed from around the world (a significant proportion were from North America). Among the items surveyed, several related to busyness and overload. Zigarelli found that a significant percentage of Christians admitted that they often or always 'rush from task to task'. He also discovered that almost 60 per cent of those surveyed confessed that the busyness of life often or always gets in the way of a relationship with God.

Zigarelli's survey did not explore the reasons for the busyness, but here is what he suggested:

> (1) Christians are assimilating to a culture of busyness, hurry and overload, which leads to (2) God becoming more marginalized in Christians' lives, which leads to (3) a deteriorating relationship with God, which leads to (4) Christians becoming even more vulnerable to adopting secular assumptions about how to live, which leads to (5) more conformity to a culture of busyness, hurry and overload. And then the cycle begins again.[103]

When our lives are so busy that we begin to feel as though we're being forced to make bricks without straw, it's perhaps not surprising if the priorities of God's kingdom begin to appear illusory. That certainly seems to have been Pharaoh's initial strategy: 'Make the work harder for the people so that they keep working and pay no attention to lies' (Exodus 5:9).

---

[103] For more, see www.christianity9to5.org/distracted-from-god/ (accessed 8th September 2020).

No wonder, then, that the leaders of the Hebrew workers turned their frustration and anger on Moses and Aaron:

> May the LORD look on you and judge you! You have made us obnoxious to Pharaoh and his officials and have put a sword in their hand to kill us.
> (Exodus 5:21)

Having taken forty years to get beyond the point where he had attempted to lead people who did not want to follow him, Moses was now faced with the reality that his leadership had effectively made things worse before they would get better. Things had been bad, but now they were unbearable. The promises of Moses appeared to be no more solid than those of a twenty-first-century politician in search of cheap votes.

Would Moses be able to hold his nerve?

In their book *Leadership on the Line*, Ronald Heifetz and Marty Linsky write about the need for leaders to 'hold steady'. The attempt to introduce significant change tends to generate resistance, and leaders need to learn to absorb their people's anger. Reflecting on this challenge, they suggest that 'exercising leadership might be understood as disappointing people at a rate they can absorb'.[104]

Even if that description of leadership might sound a little jaded, Heifetz and Linsky have a point: leaders need to hold steady when people are unhappy with the change

---

[104] Ronald A Heifetz and Marty Linsky, *Leadership on the Line: Staying Alive through the Dangers of Leading* (Boston, MA: Harvard Business Review Press, 2002), pp141-142.

they are attempting to introduce. The leader who is blown off course at the first sign of resistance is unlikely to achieve much.

So how would Moses respond to the people's negative reaction?

His response to the leaders' stinging reproach was to turn to the Lord in a way that might shock us by its frankness.

> Why, Lord, why, have you brought trouble on
> this people? Is this why you sent me? Ever since
> I went to Pharaoh to speak in your name, he has
> brought trouble on this people, and you have not
> rescued your people at all.
> (Exodus 5:22-23)

At least he was not asking for the exit: certainly not just yet.

Even though God answered him with a restatement of His promise to bring about the rescue of the Hebrews, an assurance that they would see His power, that He would take them as His people, and He would be their God, Moses was unable to communicate this to the Hebrews, so disheartened were they. They had been disappointed and their load was heavy (Exodus 6:1-9).

But the time for rescue had come. And so (after another excuse from Moses about his 'faltering lips', see Exodus 6:12) began a demonstration of God's power that would eventually break the resistance of Pharaoh and allow the Israelites to plunder the Egyptians and cross the Red Sea en route to the land of promise.

Still not convinced

God's dramatic intervention on behalf of the people got them out of Egypt, but the fact that they had witnessed such a powerful demonstration of God's power was not enough to convince the people that they could henceforth have confidence in Moses (and in the Lord) on their journey to Canaan. It didn't take long for complaints to be heard.

In the text of Exodus, hardly had the sounds of the songs of Moses and Miriam faded (Exodus 15:1-18, 21) than they were replaced with the sounds of grumbling. Over the course of several chapters, and on into the book of Numbers, Moses (and Aaron) would be the targets of repeated grumbling: lightning rods. Often it had to do with food or water, but there would also be challenges to Moses' leadership, and the disastrous rejection of the opportunity to take possession of the Promised Land, a rejection that would lead to forty years of wilderness wandering.

Commentators have observed that the first wave of grumblings (before the incident with the golden calf, in Exodus 32) was based on genuine need, while complaints in the later episodes tended to be illegitimate.[105] Not only is that a helpful observation on the text, but it's also a reminder to leaders that not every complaint (even if it is delivered in a whining tone) lacks a legitimate reason. Wise leaders will be able to discern what lies behind complaints, and when there are legitimate needs to be met,

---

[105] See Walter Kaiser, *Exodus* in *The Expositor's Bible Commentary* (Grand Rapids, MI: Zondervan, 2008; revised edition), p453.

they will pay attention to them. Complaint and criticism may turn out to be windows into the hearts of critics.

A friend once told me about an incident that had occurred when he was a young minister. On his first Sunday in the church he took out his guitar to lead the congregation in singing the chorus, 'Rejoice in the Lord Always':[106] it was probably pretty cutting edge, as this was the 1970s! An older member of the congregation became visibly unhappy and eventually left the service.

Sensibly, my friend decided to visit the man and discovered that there was a story. The man had previously donated an electronic organ to the church in memory of his late wife: when my friend introduced the guitar, the man assumed that was the end of the electronic organ. My friend observed that there is often a story behind an outburst. As leadership guru Fred Smith wisely observed, 'criticism might be an invitation to meet someone at a place of deep need'.[107]

Bitter waters

The first episode – at a location called Marah (Exodus 15), a place whose water was bitter and undrinkable, possibly because of the presence of mineral salts – came after several days of travelling in the desert, and was quickly dealt with. Moses cried to the Lord and the problem was solved when he threw a tree or a piece of wood into the water (v25). While there is evidence of Arabs putting thorn

---

[106] Lyricist unknown.
[107] Fred Smith, 'The Care and Feeding of Critics: How to Feed the Hand that Bites You', *Leadership*, 16:1, Winter 1995, p30.

bushes into some water to make it more drinkable,[108] the text tells us nothing about the healing properties of the particular tree God directed Moses to use. Moses had turned to God and God had provided a solution to his problem. Just as He had rescued Israel from the bitterness of their experience in Egypt (Exodus 1:14), so now He had rescued them from the bitterness of undrinkable water.[109]

Grumbling about food

However, it wouldn't be long before the grumbling would re-emerge. This time (Exodus 16) the whole congregation was united in grumbling against Moses and Aaron: the issue was food rather than water. Not only was food scarce in the desert, but suddenly, as Walter Kaiser puts it, 'Egypt seems all peaches and cream (actually pots of meat and all you could eat – in their idiom) rather than bondage and slave drivers'.[110] Further on in the story (Numbers 11:5), we get more detail about the Egyptian menu: 'fish … cucumbers, melons, leeks, onions and garlic'. In the eyes of the people, far from providing them with immediate relief, this leader had once again made things worse.

Without any record of Moses praying on this occasion, the Lord promised to 'rain down bread from heaven' (Exodus 16:4).

We've already seen in a previous chapter that the manna would become an object lesson in trust and dependence in the extended education programme that

---

[108] See Kaiser, *Exodus*, p454.
[109] See Alexander, *Exodus*, p312.
[110] Kaiser, *Exodus*, p457.

was an integral part of Israel's wilderness experience: always enough, but just enough for one day at a time. As Moses would later say:

> He humbled you, causing you to hunger and then feeding you with manna, which neither you nor your ancestors had known, to teach you that man does not live on bread alone but on every word that comes from the mouth of the LORD. (Deuteronomy 8:3)

But what about the grumbling? Moses and Aaron made the astute and uncomfortable assertion that the issue was not that the people were grumbling against them: after all, who were they in all of this (Exodus 16:8)? The real object of the people's grumbling was the Lord, and this would be underlined when the Lord demonstrated His glory.

That sounds like one way to silence criticism: it's not me that you're criticising, it's the Lord.

Much later in Israel's story, David was on the run from Saul. He had two opportunities to take his future into his own hands by putting an end to Saul's life. His companions reckoned such a course of action would have been a 'no-brainer'. Was it not obvious that the Lord was handing David's adversary into his hand? David stopped short of killing Saul, but cut a corner from his robe. Then, 'conscience-stricken', he said, 'The LORD forbid that I should do such a thing to my master, the LORD's anointed, or lay my hand on him; for he is the anointed of the LORD' (1 Samuel 24:5-6).

If you were ever looking for a verse that could be misappropriated to bolster your position as a spiritual leader and suppress all dissent, this, say, taken alongside Hebrews 13:17, with its injunction to submit to the authority of your leaders, would fit the bill. How dare anyone even speak against the Lord's anointed? Criticise the leader, and you are criticising the Lord Himself!

However, in reflecting more carefully on what Moses and Aaron said, we should notice that they were not attempting to secure their own leadership positions. At the end of the day, this was not about them, and therein lies an important lesson for leaders who are faced with conflict and criticism.

One of the traps for insecure leaders is to make everything about them: it is all personal. It is not always easy to separate who we are from what we do – that's what makes some criticism seem so devastating – but if I make every issue about me and interpret every criticism as personal rejection, I simply feed my insecurity and dismantle the possibility for constructive debate.

However, while that much is true, perhaps there is some apostolic precedent for self-defence in part of what Paul writes in 2 Corinthians where he mounts a fairly robust defence of his ministry, seemingly in the face of rivals who would have loved to discredit him. Discrediting Paul would have made it easier to discredit his message, thus enticing the Corinthians to drift from their devotion to Christ.

Rather than defend himself by listing his triumphs, however, Paul listed the severe challenges he had had to face; he emphasised his weakness, recounting the time when he escaped from Damascus in a basket, and the famous thorn in the flesh episode (2 Corinthians 11:33;

151

12:7). Paul knew that ultimately he was accountable to God, and the motivation for his defending himself was for the strengthening of the Corinthians.

Problems arise, however, when the necessary defence of people's well-being is confused with the leader's self-defence. It is a subtle and dangerous trap.

Don Carson makes this probing observation:

> Sadly too many leaders consciously or unconsciously link their own careers and reputations with the gospel they proclaim and the people they serve. Slowly, unnoticed by all but the most discerning, defence of the truth slips into self-defence, and the best interest of the congregation becomes identified with the best interest of the leaders.[111]

Leaders need to be aware of the danger of this subtle slide.

To return briefly to the grumbling opponents of Moses and Aaron, it needs to be said that a perpetually grumbling and complaining spirit is a sign of spiritual disorder. Grumbling is often a sign of entitlement and the antithesis of gratitude. It is the enemy of contentment and a killer of joy.

And, after all, who is it, ultimately, that we grumble against?

---

[111] D A Carson, *A Model of Christian Maturity* (Grand Rapids, MI: Baker Books, 2007), p171.

Putting God to the test

The language is stronger when we reach Exodus 17. Again there was no water. Again the people turned on Moses. But this time they *quarrelled* rather than merely grumbled (v2). Desmond Alexander notes the legal overtones to the word and comments that 'the Israelites accuse Moses of having deliberately acted against their well-being. Moses must bear responsibility for their plight'.[112]

This time there is no mention of Aaron to share the load, and Moses felt the intensity of the pressure, even beginning to wonder about his own safety in the face of the people's accusations. As he had done at Marah, he cried out to the Lord, who answered with instructions to strike the rock: water would flow from the rock and the people's need would be met.

Massah and Meribah, the twin names that Moses gave to the place where all this happened would later become bywords for faithlessness. They translate as 'testing' and 'quarrelling'. The name Meribah appears again in Numbers 20 in another incident involving a rock – an incident to which we will return towards the end of the chapter. Both names occur again in Psalm 95, a wonderful exposition of what it means to worship God that also calls on the worshippers not to harden their hearts, and it is in this context that the psalm mentions Meribah and Massah, where the people tested the Lord. As Exodus 17:7 notes, 'they tested the LORD saying, "Is the LORD among us or not?"'

---

[112] Alexander, *Exodus*, p334.

While these three episodes in Exodus are all born from legitimate concerns – people needed to be able to eat and drink in order to survive – they reveal the impatience and faithlessness of the people with whom Moses was going to have to spend the next forty years. Those leadership years would be no picnic. How do you lead people who don't merely reject your leadership, but who have little appetite for trusting God?

Onions and garlic

When we jump ahead to the narrative of the book of Numbers, we discover that the grumbling has continued, and that some of the reasons behind it have become more personal.

One of my favourite Indian meals is garlic chilli chicken, though my wife has tended to be a bit cautious about me eating it on a Saturday evening if I am preaching on Sunday morning: she's not sure that the strong smell of garlic is ideal.

Numbers 11 tells us that the Israelites missed the garlic (and fish, onions, cucumbers, melons and leeks) of Egypt. The regular menu of manna had become boring – the same plain food every day would tend that way: many of us take the variety available to us far too much for granted – and, at the instigation of a 'rabble' who were travelling with them, they began to think back to the good old days of Egypt with all that tasty free food. Yes, they ate fish 'at no cost' (Numbers 11:5)!

They say that nostalgia is a thing of the past and that the past is not what it used to be. While it's true that our minds can sometimes struggle to get beyond some of the negative episodes of our past, we also have the capacity to produce our own highlight reel of a bygone era where the sun shone more often, everyone was more pleasant and life was more civilised.

To say that the fish of Egypt had been available for free was serious revisionism.

The sound of the people wailing and the realisation of the Lord's anger troubled Moses. As we noted previously, Moses engaged in an intensely honest conversation with God. What had he done to deserve this treatment? If this is how it's going to be, where is the exit?

God's solution, as we have seen, was to allow Moses to share the load with others. In addition, He would supplement the manna with meat: quail would fall on the camp. However, while the people would get the meat they craved, they would get so much of it that they would come to loathe it (v20). The judgement for their complaining was to have too much of the thing they thought they wanted.

Let's go back to Egypt

But Egypt was not yet out of their systems. A desire to go back features in Numbers 14 as the people responded to the report from the spies that while the Promised Land was wonderful, there was no way they would be able to capture it: its people were too powerful.

This was devastating news. After leaving what had been familiar (once again, they had filtered out the worst parts) and enduring the hardships of the wilderness, it appeared that it had all been in vain. Death in Egypt or even death in the wilderness would have been preferable to the death by the sword that doubtless awaited them in Canaan. Find a leader, and let's go back!

Once again Moses and Aaron were the lightning rods, though this time they had the support of Joshua and Caleb. It might have been the end for Moses had the Lord not intervened (v10), but it was the end, for this generation, of the promise of a new place to live. Their refusal to trust the God who had broken the power of Egypt, separated the waters of the Red Sea and provided water from a rock and bread from heaven meant that they were condemned to forty years of wilderness wandering. Sadly, they would eventually drag Moses down, and in the end he would never see the successful completion of what he had begun.

When the team fragments

In between these two episodes was an attack on Moses from some of those closest to him: Miriam and Aaron (Numbers 12). Up to this point Aaron tended to be lumped with Moses as the target of the people's complaints, and just a couple of chapters further on, in chapter 14, he would once again be on the receiving end. But here, along with their sister Miriam (the Hebrew of the text suggests she took the lead), he turned on his brother.

Leaders need to be ready to hear criticism from those closest to them. It's possible to surround yourself with 'yes' men and women with the result that you never hear any negative voices, but a true partner will not be afraid to speak the truth when you need to hear it. It can be painful. The wounds of a friend may be faithful (Proverbs 27:6, ESV), but they are still wounds. As a leader, I have been on the receiving end of such wounds and I am grateful for friends who cared too much for me to leave difficult things unsaid. Sometimes it's with trembling that a faithful friend speaks to a leader: they love the leader so much that they hate to wound them, but they love them too much to leave unsaid what needs to be said.

While some of the details of the content of Miriam and Aaron's challenge are not clear, it must have been very painful for Moses to find himself treated in this way by his siblings. Norman Cohen points out that it is difficult to lead from within a hierarchy – a family hierarchy, in Moses' case – and notes that it's 'especially difficult for leaders who are younger siblings'.[113]

The text observes somewhat enigmatically that the starting point for the dispute had something to do with Moses' 'Cushite wife' (Numbers 12:1). Was this a concern for ethnic purity? Had Moses married outside his people? Does the mention of Cush suggest that this was a wife other than Zipporah from Midian? Or, as a reading of Habakkuk 3:7 might suggest, is Cush here identified with Midian?

There's an intriguing suggestion in Jewish tradition that in fact Moses' marriage to his Cushite wife had ended, owing to the demands of his leadership role and his need to be 'on call', ready to listen to God at all times. Miriam and Aaron's point (so the argument goes) was that if they could prophesy while still being married, why did Moses think he could justify separating from his wife? What

---

[113] Cohen, *Moses and the Journey to Leadership*, p123.

made him more special than them? That would certainly make sense of verse 2, when they asked, 'Has the LORD spoken only through Moses? … Hasn't he also spoken through us?'

At any rate, mention of his wife is but the prelude to their attack on Moses and his apparent uniqueness. Was this reflective of a degree of aloofness on the part of Moses? Scholars have suggested that he had never fully integrated, or that his power was ebbing and he was out of touch with the people.[114] Was this part of the reason his siblings challenged him?

Some leaders appear to be 'more comfortable on the top of the mountain than down below with the people'.[115] Leaders who are not well integrated with the group should not be surprised if people struggle to connect with their leadership. On the other hand, a leader may need to occupy a slightly different place in order to see things from a different perspective from the rest of the group.

At the end of the day, whatever faults Miriam and Aaron may have seen in Moses, was the basis of their attack on him much more than simple jealousy? In their eyes, he had no right to consider himself different from them. God had also spoken through them, had He not?

How should a leader respond when they are challenged about who they think they are?

As with any criticism, especially if it comes from a significant source, the wise leader needs to examine what's been said for even a grain of truth. Sometimes (perhaps not often), 'Who do you think you are?' is the

---

[114] Brown, *Leadership in the Wilderness*, p121.
[115] Cohen, *Moses and the Journey to Leadership*, p125.

precise question a leader needs to hear: their pride needs to be punctured and their aloofness needs to be challenged. But at other times, as was the case with Miriam and Aaron, the question is fuelled by personal jealousy. The temptation for the leader is to resort to self-defence and self-justification, and in so doing, they run the risk of being drawn into a petty personal conflict.

So what do we see in Moses?

We know that Moses could get angry. It's not long since we saw him arguing passionately with God about the perceived unfairness of the load that had been placed on his shoulders. Previously he had killed an Egyptian (Exodus 2:12), he had dealt with the men who were harassing Jethro's daughters (Exodus 2:17), and had smashed the stone tablets of the Law and ground the golden calf to powder, which he sprinkled on the water before making the Israelites drink it (Exodus 32:19-20). How would he respond to this most personal of criticisms?

The answer is, he would do nothing. It was God who intervened, summoning Miriam and Aaron and affirming that there was indeed something special about their brother. He was no ordinary prophet, to whom God spoke in visions and dreams: God spoke to Moses face to face.

Miriam was afflicted with leprosy; Aaron, humbly and desperately, asked Moses for mercy.

In the middle of all of this, we read this comment about Moses: 'Now Moses was a very humble man, more humble than anyone else on the face of the earth' (Numbers 12:3).

Assuming it was inserted by a narrator other than Moses, this gives us an insight into the effect of the leadership journey on Moses' character. English translations tend to use a word such as 'meek' or 'humble' to describe him. However, it has been suggested that a better translation might be 'miserable', with the emphasis not so much on a character attribute as on the downtrodden state in which the weight of criticism had left him.[116] In contrast, Dennis Cole notes the element of humility that is expressed in 'devout dependence on the Lord'.[117]

However we understand the term, there is no record of Moses responding to his siblings' charge: it was God who defended him.

We've already discussed the issue of self-defence on the part of leaders, and here is another ingredient for our thinking. Sometimes leaders need to leave space and time for God to vindicate them.

You may have heard or read the story that R T Kendall tells about his life-changing conversation with Josef Tson. Something had happened (we are not told what) to deeply hurt him, and Kendall was struggling with anger and bitterness. When he shared his story with his friend, Tson told him, 'R.T., you must totally forgive them. Unless you

---

[116] See Cleon Rogers, 'Moses: Meek or Miserable?', *The Journal of the Evangelical Theological Society*, September 1986, pp257-263. Used with permission.

[117] R Dennis Cole, *Numbers: An Exegetical and Theological Exposition of Holy Scripture* (Nashville, TN: Broadman & Holman, 2000), p202.

totally forgive them you will be in chains. Release them and you will be released.'[118]

Moses displayed grace when he prayed for the Lord to heal his sister. Despite what she had said to him, and the small rebellion she had initiated, she was forgiven and reintegrated into the group.

There is a wonderful scene in the first season of the TV series *The West Wing*, where Leo McGarry, the White House Chief of Staff, meets a young staff worker called Karen who has leaked personal information about him to his opponents, and has been fired for her behaviour. As they talk, and come to better understand each other, McGarry offers Karen the opportunity to have her job back, and suggests they give each other the opportunity of a new start.[119]

Grace in a powerful leader, even in the fictional Leo McGarry, is a beautiful thing. That is what Moses demonstrated.

Who do you think you are?

But it would not be long before Moses would have to face another attack on his status as leader. This time the source was Korah, along with a band of some 250 community leaders: not so much a challenge from his inner circle this time, but a challenge from members of his team. The old question resurfaced: Who do Moses and Aaron think they are?

---

[118] R T Kendall, *Total Forgiveness: Achieving God's Greatest Challenge* (London: Hodder & Stoughton, 2001), p1.
[119] 'Take Out the Trash Day', *The West Wing*, Season One, Episode 13.

> You have gone too far! The whole community is
> holy, every one of them, and the LORD is with
> them. Why then do you set yourselves above the
> LORD's assembly?
> (Numbers 16:3)

As before, Moses did not fight back to defend himself, although this time he was angry at the stubborn resistance of Korah's associates, Dathan and Abiram. But he left room for God to decide the rights and wrongs of the case. God answered, dramatically, and in chapter 17 went further to silence the wave of complaints about leadership through the miracle of the budding staff.

In thinking about Moses' remarkable restraint and humility in responding to these challenges, I wonder how much of it was a result of not having grasped leadership for himself, but instead having a very clear sense that leadership was given (and could be removed) by the Lord. Are those who have not gone after leadership for their own advancement, but who have received it as a gift from God, more likely to display grace when they are under attack? Perhaps it's those whose personal ambition has led them to pursue leadership for its power and status who are more likely to make every challenge about themselves.

Water from the rock

I will be returning to this episode from Numbers 20 in the next chapter and again in the epilogue, but I need to say something about it in the context of this chapter, for it marks the point at which Moses eventually broke. Previously the pressure had been massive, but he'd known how to turn to God, or God had stepped in to vindicate him: this time he snapped, and in so doing forfeited his place in the Promised Land.

Rather than obey the Lord's instruction to *speak* to the rock (v8), Moses spoke angrily to the people, made himself the issue ('must *we* bring you water out of this rock?',[120] v10) and *struck* the rock (twice). Despite the fact that his alternative strategy worked, God admonished him (vv11-12).

While we might have expected God to rebuke Moses for his anger, or for the harsh way he branded the Israelites as rebels, He instead focused on Moses' lack of trust and his failure to honour Him as holy (v12); later (v24) the text refers to his (and Aaron's) rebellion against God's command. Simply speaking to the rock would have upheld the holiness and majesty of God who would have been seen as the true provider of water. Timothy Ashley comments:

> Instead, by their lack of reliance on Yahweh, they have proved to be impediments to the manifestation of Yahweh's power and holiness before the eyes of his people. When this happens, leaders of God's people have lost their ability to lead.[121]

---

[120] Emphasis mine.

[121] Timothy R Ashley, *The Book of Numbers*, The New International Commentary on the Old Testament (Grand Rapids, MI: Eerdmans, 1993), p386.

Ironically, the rebellious unbelief that had barred the wilderness generation from Canaan had done the same for Moses and Aaron.

The book of Psalms adds this fascinating commentary on the incident:

> By the waters of Meribah they angered the LORD,
> and trouble came to Moses because of them;
> for they rebelled against the Spirit of God,
> and rash words came from Moses' lips.
> (Psalm 106:32-33).

The ESV construes things slightly differently, opting to interpret 'Spirit of God' as the spirit of Moses: 'they made his spirit bitter'.

It's possible to argue that no one else can make you angry. They may provoke you, but it's your choice to respond in anger. I understand why people say that: it counters the temptation to shift responsibility for our actions and behaviour. However, while it's certainly true that the Lord held Moses responsible for what he did, Psalm 106 recognises that there were mitigating circumstances: there will be times when leaders feel that they have borne more than enough.

Leaders need to know themselves, recognise their trigger points and put a guard around themselves, especially in those moments of weariness or provocation. Criticism and conflict may come with the job, but if they are handled badly they can spell serious trouble for the leader and for their legacy.

Four key implications

Our survey of the grumbling and criticism that Moses had to face through much of his leadership throws up a whole set of important issues for any of us involved in leadership, and it will be helpful to review four of them before leaving the chapter.

First, leaders need to learn to distinguish between the kind of conflict and critique that are probably necessary if they are to grow as leaders, and harsh, personal criticism from professional fault-finders. If we don't get this right we will either be crushed and our leadership will become anaemic (if indeed we remain in leadership), or we will become stubborn and our leadership will be blinkered.

Leadership scholar Dennis Tourish has argued that 'the most successful leaders are liable to be those with the least compliant followers'.[122] At first glance this seems to fly in the face of the suggestion that leaders need their followers to be fully aligned with the goals of the organisation, but in fact it underlines the idea that healthy leadership will welcome rather than attempt to quash alternative perspectives.

Second, there may be times when leaders find themselves attempting to lead people who have no wish to follow their leadership – indeed, in terms of spiritual leadership, some of them may have lost their appetite for following God. To be realistic, it's unlikely that you will always enjoy a 100 per cent approval rating. When people don't want to follow you, you can try to force them into

---

[122] Dennis Tourish, *The Dark Side of Transformational Leadership: A Critical Perspective* (Hove: Routledge, 2013), p87.

line by flexing your muscles or through manipulation. Perhaps, for a time, you will silence your critics and create something that looks like silent compliance. But how much better would it be, even if it takes longer, to cultivate consistency and character rather than attempt to build your leadership credibility on a foundation of power?

Then leaders need to know how to hold their nerve. At times, particularly when a church or organisation needs to undergo a radical overhaul, things may seem to get worse before they get better. If you are convinced that the direction is right and your motivation is right, then hold your nerve. No doubt there are plenty of stubborn leaders who refuse to alter course when they really should, but there are times when leaders need to persevere in the direction they believe they have discerned from God.

Finally, remember that leadership is a sacred trust: one of the biggest traps is to make everything about you (sometimes that's the agenda that the critics set) and to forget that what you have has been given by God. Fall into that trap, like Moses, and you jeopardise your legacy.

Over it all, remember that the God who has entrusted your leadership to you stands with you to sustain you and vindicate you in His time.

Questions for reflection

- Do you tend to see conflict and criticism as painful experiences to be avoided, or do you welcome them as pathways to growth and greater self-awareness?

- How can leaders discern between times when they need to change course and times when they need to hold their nerve?

- How strong is your conviction that your leadership has been given to you as a sacred trust? What difference does this make to how you lead?

7

Wise Leaders Realise That They Are Not the Finished Article

Then Moses raised his arm and struck the rock twice with his staff.
(Numbers 20:11)

In his book *Redefining Leadership*, Joseph Stowell describes two types of leader. The first are what he calls 'outcome-driven' leaders: as the description suggests, the focus of their leadership is on maximising outcomes and their ability to produce results. 'Character-driven leaders' (or 'kingdom leaders'), on the other hand, while still committed to good outcomes, focus on the importance of developing their character.

He writes:

> It's our upside-down-ness that leads us to think that successful leaders are measured by the size and scope of the enterprise, its branding, its national and even international acclaim, its

profitability, the fame and platform of the leader.[123]

In contrast, the Lord is interested 'in who the leader is at the core and how he or she is leading as a steward of the work of the kingdom'.[124]

Leadership is not simply a matter of results, of goals met, of vision realised, of measurable growth and progress. Important as all of these are, who you are as a leader matters. As Paul Tripp has reminded us in a recent book on church leadership, 'Achievement becomes dangerous when it controls our definition of leaders.'[125]

Who you are matters because who you are can shape your leadership for good or ill. When leaders' character flaws begin to seep out into their leadership, trust is lost and leadership is easily blown off course.

But character also matters because God is more interested in who we are than in what we do. We are called to be holy, and spiritual leadership, like all of life, has His glory as its goal. It's sobering to realise that while Moses' act of striking the rock in Numbers 20 brought about the desired outcome (water), God was more concerned about what was essentially a failure of character. We need more than pragmatism: we need more than simply the pursuit of what works. Outcomes cannot tell the whole story.

But what, exactly, is character?

---

[123] Joseph M Stowell, *Redefining Leadership: Character-Driven Habits of Effective Leaders* (Grand Rapids, MI: Zondervan, 2014), p18.
[124] Ibid, p18.
[125] Tripp, *Lead*, p38.

While there may be an overlap or interconnection between character and personality, they are not the same, and some of the distinctions are important. Much of our personality is morally neutral. For example, there is nothing inherently more upright about being an introvert than an extrovert; someone who loves to get absorbed in drawing up and following detailed plans is not necessarily more saintly than someone who prefers spontaneity. Character, on the other hand, includes aspects that are value-laden.

Os Guinness suggests that character is 'the essential "stuff" a person is made of, the inner reality and quality in which thoughts, speech, decisions, behavior, and relations are rooted'.[126]

The Bible and character

Unsurprisingly, Scripture, in both Old and New Testaments, places great emphasis on the importance of character.

Old Testament writers exhort the people of God as a whole to be obedient, and call them to live in holiness, a reflection of the holiness of God. More specifically, and with reference to leaders, special attention was given to Israel's kings. Deuteronomy 17 highlights three specific areas to which kings needed to pay careful attention: military (the reference to horses, v16), political (the reference to wives, v17, doubtless 'acquired' in the process

---

[126] Os Guinness, ed, *Character Counts: Leadership Qualities in Washington, Wilberforce, Lincoln, and Solzhenitsyn* (Grand Rapids, MI: Baker, 1999), p12.

of establishing political alliances) and economic (the reference to wealth, v17). There is nothing new about the lure of money, sex and power. As Gordon McConville observes in his commentary on Deuteronomy, the three spheres of temptation would normally have been viewed as areas by which to measure the success of a king.[127] Further on in this chapter, we will observe the deep irony in the fact that apparent success can contain within it the seeds of failure.

The New Testament continues the emphasis on character, whether in the general application of Jesus' Sermon on the Mount (Matthew 5–7), in Paul's list of the qualities that mark the person who is led by the Spirit – the fruit of the Spirit – and which reflect the character of Christ (Galatians 5:22-23), or in the specific qualities that relate to church leaders as they are outlined in the letters to Timothy and Titus.

The teaching of Jesus puts the focus firmly on the inner world of motives and desires. It's not just the act of murder; it's the heart filled with angry scorn. It's not just the act of adultery; it's the adulterous heart. It's not external traditions that make us clean; the issue is the disordered world of our heart: it is 'out of the abundance of the heart [the] mouth speaks' (Luke 6:45, ESV). To refer back to the Old Testament, above everything else we are to guard our hearts, for all that we do flows from them (Proverbs 4:23).

Speaker and author Paul Tripp uses a simple illustration that underlines the point. If you take a bottle

---

[127] J Gordon McConville, *Deuteronomy*, Apollos Old Testament Commentary (London: Apollos, 2002), p294.

of water, remove the lid and shake the bottle, what happens? Water comes out. But why? An obvious answer might be that you shook the bottle. But what happens if we change the emphasis and the question becomes, 'Why did *water* come out of the bottle?' The answer is '[because] water was in the bottle'.[128]

That is why our hearts matter. That is why character matters.

Yet at the same time that we have this emphasis on character and the call to be holy, Scripture is very honest about the character flaws of many of its greatest leaders. It's sobering to realise that wisdom and folly can coexist in the same human heart.

Among those flawed leaders is Moses.

Back to Meribah

It's at Meribah, in the incident we have already referred to in Chapter Six, that Moses behaved in a way that sabotaged his own leadership and disqualified him from entering the Promised Land. Pushed beyond the limit by the quarrelling of the community, something in Moses snapped and he angrily rebuked the people before taking his staff, the symbol of divine power in his ministry, and striking the rock rather than speaking to it as God had told him to (Numbers 20:2-11).

There had been a previous occasion at Rephidim (Exodus 17:6) when Moses had been correct to strike the rock with his staff. This time was to have been different.

---

[128] See www.youtube.com/watch?v=xIYX-kxeZIs (accessed 12th October, 2021).

The consequences of Moses' disobedience would be painful, leading to the deep disappointment of not being allowed to enter the land of promise. I think it was ironic that he should fail in the way that he did at Meribah, and this for at least three reasons.

A failure to trust

For one, as we have already seen, God reproached him for his unbelief (Numbers 20:12): this was the same sin that had barred the way to Canaan for an entire generation of Israelites, and now it had done so for Moses. Throughout his leadership journey, Moses had learned to trust God, to look to Him in moments of difficulty. We felt sorry for him when we realised that he was going to have to spend forty years in the desert because of the faithlessness of other people. Yet here he was, in his turn, failing to trust God.

A failure of humility

Second, we wonder about Moses' behaviour at Meribah in light of the observation in Numbers 12:3 that he was 'a very humble man, more humble than anyone else on the face of the earth': do such people give way to outbursts of anger? We've already noted the suggestion that the verse may be emphasising how miserable and downtrodden he was, rather than the quality of humility, but either reading suggests the possibility that the passage of time has allowed the cultivation of a meeker, more passive Moses: perhaps not the kind of person we'd automatically expect to get angry and smash rocks with his staff.

However, we know that Moses had previously demonstrated the capacity for anger. We can recall earlier displays, not least at injustice or unfaithfulness. The killing of an Egyptian (Exodus 2:12). The smashing of the stone tablets (Exodus 32:19). And we know that his anger re-emerged in the face of the challenge from Dathan and Abiram (Numbers 16:15), although the text explains that in this instance he took it to God.

Moses was still a work in progress, and at Meribah his anger erupted once more. But this was not righteous anger that arose out of a sense of injustice or offence that his God had been dishonoured: this time his patience had snapped and his frustration was directed at the people.

I wonder how often there are traits that we imagine have been confined to our past, tendencies that we reckon have been tempered or more or less brought under control with the passage of time and the maturing of our character, but they are still there, lurking not far from the surface. Perhaps we are not, after all, the completed article.

A failure to honour God

But a third irony, and one I want to dwell on a little, lies in the contrast between Moses' behaviour at Meribah and his response in two earlier episodes, both of them occasions when God offered to blot out the Israelites and create a nation from Moses.

The first was the incident of the golden calf (Exodus 32). In their impatience at Moses' delay in returning from Sinai, the people had managed to persuade Aaron to organise the production of an alternative deity. They worshipped this calf-shaped idol, using words that were a blasphemous parody of the preamble to the Ten Commandments: 'These are your gods, Israel, who brought you up out of Egypt' (Exodus 32:4).

Aaron then built an altar and announced 'a festival to the LORD' (v5; was this Aaron's attempt to salve his own conscience?). The religious part of the festival soon gave way to drinking and revelry, at which point God told Moses to go back down the mountain: his (Moses') people had 'become corrupt' and given themselves to idolatry (vv7-8). By now the Lord was ready to destroy the people: and ready to start again by making Moses into a 'great nation' (v10).

Moses responded in what has to be one of the finest moments of his leadership. Why would the Lord do this? Why would He give the Egyptians an excuse to question His character? He then went on to remind the Lord of His own promises to the patriarchs: how would wiping out these people reflect on those promises (vv11-13)?

The Lord relented and Moses returned to the camp. He was angry, smashing the stone tablets of the Law and destroying the calf. In a wild and violent episode, as the people ran amok, the Levites rallied to Moses and went through the camp, killing their brothers and friends: some 3,000 people were killed. Later, despite Moses' intercession, more of them died in a plague (v35).

What is remarkable is Moses' willingness to stand in the gap (see Ezekiel 22:30) between the people and God, even to the point where he was willing to have his own name blotted out of God's book (Exodus 32:32). The glory of God and the welfare of God's people mattered more to Moses than his own well-being.

The second incident comes in Numbers 14, with the people's rejection of the Promised Land. Although the land was wonderful, its people were too powerful for the Israelites to be able to displace them. At least, that's what the majority of the spies told them. Despite the impassioned appeal of the dissenting voices of Joshua and Caleb, fear and unbelief had taken deep root and the people responded with threats of violence against their leaders.

When God intervened, He was ready, as He had been at Sinai, to put an end to the people and to bring into existence another nation, starting with Moses (v12).

When you keep in mind the frequent carping and complaining that had been directed at Moses, this might sound like an offer that he would have been crazy to refuse. The grumbling voices would be silenced. Life and leadership would be so much easier. How would you have responded had you been in Moses' position and the offer had been made to you?

It's not that Christian leaders should be in the business of calling for plagues on troublemakers(!), but how many leaders would be overjoyed if God announced that He was going to relocate some of their critics to the church down the road, or arrange their transfer to a faraway country? Just give God a list of the ten people who are holding you back, and once He has moved them along, you can enjoy some distraction-free leadership!

Some of us would find it difficult to turn down an offer like that.

But that is not at all how Moses responded.

> Then the Egyptians will hear about it! By your
> power you brought these people up from among
> them. And they will tell the inhabitants of this
> land about it. They have already heard that you,
> LORD, are with these people ... the nations who
> have heard this report about you will say, 'The
> LORD was not able to bring these people into the
> land he promised them on oath, so he
> slaughtered them in the wilderness.'
> (Numbers 14:13-16)

Far from reaching for the promise of a glorious and comfortable future for himself, Moses was focused on the reputation of the Lord. The nations needed to know that what they had heard about this unique God, who had travelled with His people and who had been known among them, was true. He was as powerful as they thought. When you see a leader whose focus is God's honour more than their own, you see a leader whose heart is in the right place and whose character has begun to mature.

I think we see an echo of this quality in the attitude of Paul when he writes to the church in Philippi about people who are preaching the gospel and advancing their ministry while he is chained up as a prisoner. Sure, their motives are terrible – they are hoping to make things worse for Paul – but the result is that 'Christ is preached', and for Paul that's what really matters (Philippians 1:15-18).

If your ministry or your leadership is primarily about you and your reputation, that's what will govern your decision-making. You will be tempted to take the path that shows you in the best light or that makes your life most comfortable. Don't be surprised when, sooner or later, you lose your way. On the other hand, if your leadership is genuinely about God, you will be willing to put up with a great deal as long as He is honoured.

These two incidents point to the fact that in his finest moments, Moses put God's honour and reputation above his own advancement. That's why it is so ironic that at Meribah he made himself the centre of attention and failed to honour God. How sad that in the very area where he had been at his best, he had his most grievous fall.

Not the finished article

Wise leaders have learned that they are not the finished article. Even if we manage to rein in our most destructive impulses, and even if by the grace of God we undergo a degree of deep-rooted character change, we do well to heed the warning: those who think they are standing firm must be wary of the danger of falling (1 Corinthians 10:12). As author Jerry Bridges reminded us:

> Your worst days are never so bad that you are beyond the *reach* of God's grace. And your best days are never so good that you are beyond the *need* of God's grace.[129]

---

[129] Jerry Bridges, *The Discipline of Grace: God's Role and Our Role in the Pursuit of Holiness* (Colorado Springs, CO: NavPress, 1994), p18.

How is it that we can be such a mixture of nobility and shame, of wisdom and folly? Dr Edward John Carnell, a former president of Fuller Seminary in California, once said that 'the self is a swirling conflict of fears, impulses, sentiments, interests, allergies, and foibles'.[130] Only God can fully discern what is going on within each of us.

But how often do we pause long enough even to attempt to figure out what is going on inside us? To borrow from Parker Palmer:

> Those of us who readily embrace leadership, especially public leadership, tend toward extroversion, which often means ignoring what is happening inside ourselves. If we have any sort of inner life, we 'compartmentalize' it, walling it off from our public work. This, of course, allows the shadow to grow unchecked until it emerges, larger than life, in the public realm.[131]

He goes on to write about how we tend to shy away from embarking on an inner journey that might force us to confront the hardest realities of our lives: it's a lot easier to spend our time focused on our external world.

Wise leaders are well aware that inner work remains to be done.

Moses is by no means alone in Scripture's catalogue of incomplete and flawed leaders: no doubt you can think of

---

[130] Quoted in an article by Ray Ortlund: see www.thegospelcoalition.org/blogs/ray-ortlund/edward-john-carnell-1919-1967/ (accessed 8th February 2021).
[131] Palmer, *Let Your Life Speak*, p79.

several others. There are kings like David, a man 'after [God's] own heart' (1 Samuel 13:14), associated with so much of the most precious writing in the Bible, who committed adultery and arranged for the death of the man whose wife he had taken (2 Samuel 11). There's Hezekiah, an essentially good king, until he allowed his pride to get the better of him and showed off his treasure house to Babylonian envoys (2 Kings 20:12-15). Think of Peter, who was able to move almost instantaneously from expressing the God-given insight that Jesus was the Christ, to attempting to dissuade Jesus from the path to the cross (Matthew 16:13-23). Later, even as a significant leader in the early Church, Peter had to be publicly reprimanded by Paul for his hypocrisy (Galatians 2:11-14). Paul himself, such a massive figure in the spread of the gospel, and such a shaper of Christian thought, had a deep falling-out with his friend Barnabas (one of the most gracious leaders in the New Testament – though apparently he was not exempt from the influence of Peter's hypocrisy: Acts 15:39; Galatians 2:13). Was this the same Paul that wrote about love in 1 Corinthians 13? These are not picture-perfect saints. None of us is the completed article: character is a work in progress.

Earlier in the chapter we noted Deuteronomy's warning for kings about horses, wives and wealth. Success, whether economic, political or military, can be part of the pathway to ruin.

No Israelite king had success like Solomon: here is how 1 Kings describes his success:

> King Solomon was greater in riches and wisdom
> than all the other kings of the earth ... everyone

who came brought a gift – articles of silver and gold, robes, weapons and spices, and horses and mules.

Solomon accumulated chariots and horses; he had fourteen hundred chariots and twelve thousand horses ... The king made silver as common in Jerusalem as stones, and cedar as plentiful as sycamore-fig trees in the foothills. Solomon's horses were imported from Egypt.

(1 Kings 10:23-28)

Was this prosperity not a sign of God's blessing? After all, when Solomon had asked God for wisdom to rule well, God had promised what he asked for, and promised to add wealth and honour: Solomon would have no equal among kings (2 Chronicles 1:7-12).

Clearly there is a balance to be found: while wealth can be a sign of the blessing of God (not least in the Old Testament era) its danger is that it can turn the heart of its possessor away from God. It's often been pointed out that it is not money itself, but the love of it, that is 'a root of all kinds of evil' (1 Timothy 6:10). Wealth carries an allure. We can set our hearts on it and we can put our hope in it. Yet it can be fickle. Jesus calls us not to 'store up ... treasures on earth' and Paul warns that those who want to get rich fall into a trap (Matthew 6:19; 1 Timothy 6:9).

Deuteronomy's warning about horses appears to have related particularly to Egypt (where Solomon sourced some of his). Commentator Peter Craigie wonders if the issue might have been that the acquisition of horses involved a trade-off in terms of Israelite soldiers, in which case Israelites who ought to have been free would have been back working in Egypt.[132] Whether or not he is correct, Egypt represented the past for the people of God, and they were not to go back (Deuteronomy 17:16).

Christian leaders tend not to measure the extent of their power by numbers of horses or chariots, but we still like to measure our achievements. How many churches have an annual health check that involves numbers? Seats filled, members added, decisions for Christ, money donated to mission. These are not bad things, but we do well to check our hearts for the presence of symptoms such as pride and an inappropriate self-confidence: signs, perhaps, that our success and our status have begun to go to our heads.

What about Solomon's wives?

> King Solomon, however, loved many foreign women besides Pharaoh's daughter ... Solomon held fast to them in love ... and his wives led him astray. As Solomon grew old, his wives turned his heart after other gods, and his heart was not fully devoted to the LORD his God, as the heart of David his father had been.
> (1 Kings 11:1-4)

Whatever political purpose these marriages served (and there were a lot of them), these were affairs of the heart. Solomon loved these women. How ironic that the man who warned his son to guard his heart, for everything else would flow from it (Proverbs 4:23), failed to guard his

---

[132] Peter C Craigie, *The Book of Deuteronomy*, The New International Commentary on the Old Testament (Grand Rapids, MI: Eerdmans, 1976), pp255-256.

own. Rather than being marked by growth in devotion to the Lord, his later years were stained by the lure of the false gods of the women he loved.

Leaders – men and women – need to recognise their areas of vulnerability. Remember, none of us is the completed article.

Isn't it striking that there are things which might appear to be the measures of success, but within them they carry the seeds of leadership failure?

Reflect for a moment on how success is measured in your sphere of leadership. It's perfectly reasonable to have measurable criteria when you, as a leader, are employed by someone and accountable to them for your work. Yet we need to acknowledge that not everything that matters can be measured.

You can count the number of people in a worship gathering, but you can't really measure the quality of the worship (saying things like, 'The worship was really good this morning,' when we are actually evaluating the band and the choice of songs, is not particularly helpful). Can you really quantify the richness of the relationships of people in your sphere of responsibility?

If it's true that what really matters cannot always be measured, it's also true that those things that can be measured easily become the things that really matter to us and our priorities become skewed: as Goodhart's Law suggests, 'When a measure becomes a target, it ceases to be a good measure.'[133]

---

[133] Named after the British economist Charles Goodhart, though the wording is believed to be attributed to a 1997 article by Marilyn

Solomon's story warns us that when our focus is on externally recognisable measures of success, we can lose sight of the character disintegration that may be taking place even as we are applauded and admired for our success.

Four considerations

So where does all of this leave us? By way of wrapping up this chapter, here are four things to which leaders (and anyone else, really) need to pay attention.

Unresolved patterns

For Moses it was anger – as it may be for you. As a leader you are used to getting your own way on all the big issues (and even on the small ones): no one stops you because they have learned to fear your anger.

Anger is a tricky emotion to handle, not least because there are times when we are guilty of not being angry enough, or rather of not being angry at things that ought to provoke it. There are times when it is not enough to shrug our shoulders: remember that some of the earliest manifestations of Moses' passion were aimed at injustice. However, Paul urges us not to sin in our anger and not to 'let the sun go down' while it is unresolved (Ephesians 4:26). James adds that we are to be slow to get angry: it will

Strathern: '"Improving rating": Audit in the British University system', *European Review* 5(3), pp305-321.

not accomplish 'the righteousness that God desires' (James 1:19-20).

Even if we're not guilty of Meribah-style rock-splitting fits of rage, some of us may be far too tolerant of a simmering self-centred impatience or a constant spirit of complaint.

For other leaders it may be pride, at times expressed in outbursts of anger, but also evident in an arrogance, or a spirit of superiority. For still others the unresolved pattern may involve lust, lurking like an untamed mountain lion in the basement. For some it's greed, self-indulgence, a hankering after comfort and luxury.

What a tragedy if these patterns are unnoticed or, perhaps worse, if they are noticed but tolerated and left unresolved until they take deeper root in our lives to the point that we have our own Meribah moment and sabotage our leadership.

Unguarded devotion

This is Solomon. The man whose writing urges us to guard our hearts left his own unguarded. Not only did he give his heart to the many foreign women who came to share his life, but he also allowed the lure of those women's gods to draw his devotion away from the Lord (1 Kings 11:4-6).

Unlike Solomon, few Christian leaders are likely to give their hearts to foreign gods, but how many will find themselves drawn to the idolatrous pursuit of popularity or success? Leaders are worshippers – we all are. The question is: what has captured our hearts and what are we doing to guard them from the allurements of misdirected affections and illegitimate gods?

Unfinished growth

Wise leaders realise that they are not the finished article. They know that there is still work to be done in the development of their character. This leads to a question: if the development of our character is still incomplete, a work in progress, what are the actual character qualities into which we should be growing? How might we measure character growth?

There are so many ways we could answer that. We could talk about what it means to be holy, as the God who called us is holy (1 Peter 1:16). We could talk about following the example of Christ (1 Corinthians 11:1), or we could reflect on the fruit of the Spirit (Galatians 5:22-23). Or we could go to Scripture's two great commandments: the command to love God and to love others (Matthew 22:37-40). As Dan Allender puts it, 'Character is grown to the degree that we love God and others.'[134]

Jesus taught that it's on these two commandments that everything else hangs (Matthew 22:40). Or, in Paul's formulation, love – which 'does no harm to a neighbour' – 'is the fulfilment of the law' (Romans 13:10).

This is the measure of our growth in character.

Do I love God more now than I did a year ago? More than ten years ago? How would I answer the question that Jesus asked Peter in John 21:15: 'do you love me more than

---

[134] Allender, *Leading With a Limp*, p145.

these?' That seemed to be Jesus' requirement for leadership.

And am I growing in my love for other people? Are my relationships marked by a greater degree of patience? Am I doing better at rejoicing at the triumphs of others? Would people say that I am more gracious and less resentful than I was ten years ago? Of course, leaders ought to be growing in knowledge, honing their gifts and developing their talents: by all means set yourself goals and targets for personal development. But would people who know you describe you as kind? For all your firmness and decisiveness as a leader, are you known as gentle? Do your people know that you have their best interest at heart?

Unsurpassable grace

Earlier in the chapter we referred to something Jerry Bridges wrote about God's grace. It bears repeating:

> Your worst days are never so bad that you are beyond the *reach* of God's grace. And your best days are never so good that you are beyond the *need* of God's grace.[135]

It's certainly another reminder that we are not the finished article, but there is also an encouragement not to give up. Just as it is grace that has brought us 'safe thus far',[136] so there is grace for the gap between where we are and where

---

[135] Bridges, *The Discipline of Grace*, p18.
[136] 'Amazing Grace', John Newton (1725-1807).

we need to reach, and there is grace for the gap between what we wish we were and what we know we still are.

Finishing well

When Dallas Seminary professor Howard Hendricks died in 2013, among the tributes that were paid was this one, from one of his students:

> I asked him, if we forgot everything else he had ever taught us (which was unlikely), what one thing would he want us to remember? He thought a moment and replied, 'Finish well.' He said plenty of people in the Bible did well for a time, but very few of them finished their lives faithfully.[137]

Wise leaders know they are not the finished article, but the humility that comes from that realisation will help them to finish well.

---

[137] www.dts.edu/howard-hendricks-tribute/ (accessed 18th November 2020).

Questions for reflection

- Are you aware of personal tendencies that could potentially shipwreck your leadership?

- Have you grown in your love for God and others in the past twelve months? Would those who know you best agree?

- What steps can you take to ensure that you finish well?

8

Wise Leaders Know How to Hand on the Baton

As I was with Moses, so I will be with you; I will never leave
you nor forsake you.
(Joshua 1:5)

Every leadership assignment has a shelf life, and no human leader gets to lead forever. Therefore it is wise to put in place what Rabbi David Baron refers to as an 'exit strategy':[138] part of that strategy involves taking steps to ensure the future well-being of the people and organisation that they have led.

Similarly, scholar and teacher Norman Cohen notes:

> Mature leaders realize when the time is near for them to leave the stage, though surrendering power is rarely easy. However, their handing

---

[138] David Baron, with Lynette Padwa, *Moses on Management: 50 Leadership Lessons from the Greatest Manager of All Time* (New York: Pocket Books, 1999), p200.

over the mantle in a gracious way is crucial for a sense of continuity.[139]

For much of the Old Testament era – the time of Israel's kings – leadership of the nation made its way from one generation of the ruling dynasty to the next. But Scripture had already shone a light on the inadequacies of family succession. In the story of Samuel, the Old Testament text describes the sons of Eli, the priest, as 'scoundrels', and Eli had long lost whatever power he had to influence them for good (1 Samuel 2:12, 25). As for Samuel himself, although he had been a good man, his attempt to appoint his sons as his successors was rejected by the elders of the people. Sadly, it turned out that his sons were far from following in his footsteps (1 Samuel 8:1-5).

There never seems to have been any question of Moses handing over the reins of leadership to either of his two sons (who largely disappear from the telling of his story). Unlike the practice of the Egyptians among whom he had grown up, he would not attempt to establish a Mosaic dynasty. Yet one of the marks of his leadership was his concern for the future of his people, a future that would extend long beyond the time of his leadership.

In Numbers 27, God told Moses that he would let him see the Promised Land before the end of his life. He would see it but never live there. There would be no reversal of the consequence of his failure to obey God at Meribah. As Moses' mind turned to the people he would leave behind, he talked to the Lord about the question of leadership succession.

---

[139] Cohen, *Moses and the Journey to Leadership*, pp165-166.

> May the LORD, the God who gives breath to all
> living things, appoint someone over this
> community to go out and come in before them,
> one who will lead them out and bring them in,
> so that the LORD's people will not be like sheep
> without a shepherd.
> (Numbers 27:16-17)

The answer to Moses' prayer was staring him in the face: Joshua, 'a man in whom is the spirit of leadership' (Numbers 27:18),[140] would become the leader of the people and Moses would commission him. In Deuteronomy 31, as the story of his leadership wound to a close, Moses summoned Joshua, urging him to 'be strong and courageous' as he led the people into Canaan and allocated their various portions to them. The Lord would go before him and be with him. He would never leave or forsake him. There was no need for him to be afraid or discouraged (v6). Later in the chapter, the Lord Himself affirmed the message to Joshua: 'Be strong and courageous, for you will bring the Israelites into the land I promised them on oath, and I myself will be with you' (Deuteronomy 31:23).

I realise that not everyone gets to choose their successor (which may not be a bad thing). Certainly in the world of local churches, few congregations belonging to established denominations operate in a way that makes it possible for a departing leader to appoint the person who will follow them. If all goes well, the outgoing leader is

---

[140] The NIV opts to interpret the verse referring to 'spirit' rather than 'Spirit', and adds the word 'leadership' which is missing in the Hebrew, though arguable in the context.

rewarded with a rousing send-off that includes tea and cake, but then it's over to someone else to appoint a successor.

Nonetheless, I would suggest that even though a leader may not always get to have a say in the appointment of their immediate successor, part of the leader's task should involve a focus on the future. It should not be unusual that a significant part of a leader's legacy is seen in the number and quality of next-generation leaders who are trained and released into their own spheres of influence.

How should leaders go about this, whether it is helping to prepare their own successor or helping to identify and prepare younger leaders who will one day be released into wider ministry? Are there particular qualities to look for in emerging leaders? And, in a related question, how can leaders prepare themselves for the day when they will hand over the baton and will no longer be in the spotlight? It's possible for a leader to mar their legacy by holding the reins for too long.

While Moses' prayer for a successor came towards the end of his life, preparations for succession had effectively been going on for some forty years. Whether or not Moses had intentionally marked Joshua out as his successor is not clear, but there is value in taking the time to review how the text of the Pentateuch describes the relationship and interaction between the two men. Sometimes it's simply in working with and observing a more experienced leader that a younger leader is shaped for their future role. Jesus not only taught by means of verbal instruction; he also taught by example.

Joshua is one of only two men (the other is Caleb) who would manage to survive the wilderness years and make it into the Promised Land. Although he is introduced to us as Joshua, we later discover that he was originally known as Hoshea, but Moses renamed him Joshua (Numbers 13:16). No specific reason for the change is given in the text, but the new name is a reminder that salvation comes from the Lord.[141]

A military assignment

Our first encounter with Joshua comes in a military context in Exodus 17, when he was tasked with leading the Israelite army in battle against the Amalekites. As Desmond Alexander notes, we're not given any particular reason why Moses entrusted him with this task.[142] We can surmise that he had displayed some leadership gifts, and it is fairly clear that Moses trusted him. Beyond his leading the army, Numbers 11:28 notes that he had been Moses' aide, or assistant, 'since youth'.

When some leaders look back over their leadership journey, it is almost as though they can hardly remember a time when they were not involved in leadership. Leadership has always felt very natural, perhaps like stepping into a comfortable pair of old slippers (not that leadership is always comfortable).

---

[141] See Ashley, *Numbers,* p233; note also the Jewish tradition that suggests Moses renamed his young protégé in a desire that he would be kept safe on his assignment as a spy.
[142] Alexander, *Exodus,* p339.

Others may look back with a degree of puzzlement: someone must have seen something in them that they did not see in themselves. Some of these people are the reluctant, or even accidental, leaders. One of the finest leaders I know, reflecting on his developing years, told me that he would describe himself as a reluctant leader; however, despite his own reticence he could see that he was often 'coughed up' into leadership positions.

What is it that people see in a young, developing leader? In the New Testament, Timothy was well spoken of by the believers who knew him before Paul decided to recruit him for mission (Acts 16:2). Later, Paul would write that he had no one else like Timothy; in contrast to others who were marked by self-interest, Timothy had a genuine concern for the welfare of others (Philippians 2:20). He had 'proved himself', serving with Paul in the mission of the gospel. He had been like a 'son with his father' (v22) – an image, as Don Carson points out, that draws on the ancient custom (less prevalent today) of sons following in the footsteps of their father's vocation.[143]

Don't rush past the fact that Timothy proved himself at home before being selected for adventures that would take him further afield, and that he proved himself with Paul before being sent to the Philippians.

So what should we be looking for in someone to whom we will hand on the baton? What are the character traits of future leaders?

To start with, we might suggest dependability: someone who turns up when they say they will and can

---

[143] D A Carson, in David Porter, ed, *Putting the Gospel First* (Leicester: Crossway Books, 1995), p54.

be relied on to work hard at their commitments. What about an eagerness to learn and a teachable spirit? A humility that nonetheless co-exists with a certain degree of boldness and confidence? Or the ability to relate well to all kinds of people? What about the ability to see clearly and act decisively? It might be evidence of loyalty to the values and mission of your organisation.

Recently, I posed the question to a friend, a freshly retired bishop. He had a good think about it and came up with a list: teachability (those who are not teachable don't learn and tend not to change), a passion for Christ, humility, openness, creativity, the testimony of their life with God, vision, the ability to make something happen, an ability to communicate and orthodoxy. The last of these may seem like a given for the Church, but it needs to be stated, for a leader's ability to be creative and imaginative comes unhinged if it is not rooted in Scripture and orthodoxy. Similarly, the 'halo effect' means that an emerging leader may dazzle in one or two areas where they are particularly strong, but this can sometimes hide weaknesses elsewhere. It's easy to be impressed by charisma, or by an apparent confidence, which may well be helpful in a leader but which doesn't tell the whole story.

In keeping with my friend's suggestion, I'd want to underline the quality of teachability. While I was writing this chapter I had a conversation with a younger – though already quite accomplished – leader. He wanted to ask me something I don't think anyone else has ever asked me: how could he intentionally leave space for the voices of those who might be critical of him or disagree with his work?

How many of us would do that? If the majority of the voices around us are positive and affirming of our work, would we not just accept them and take it as confirmation that we are doing OK? There is a humility and a courage at work in someone who knows that they need to hear dissenting voices if their leadership is to continue to grow.

That is maturity. That is the kind of humble, teachable attitude that I think marks out a young leader who is likely to go far.

Whatever it was that Moses saw in Joshua, he proves to have been a shrewd judge of leader potential.

To go back to the battle with Amalek in Exodus 17, however skilful Joshua may have been as a military leader, the narrative makes it clear that he was by no means the sole author of Israel's success. Had it not been for Moses holding up the staff of God, Joshua and the army would have been defeated. Beyond that, had it not been for Aaron and Hur helping Moses to hold his hands steady as he grew tired, the outcome would have been different. Would Joshua ever forget that lesson? Could it be that what he learned here about the Lord as the giver of victory made it easier to carry out the rather unusual strategy that brought down the walls of Jericho in Joshua 6?

Sinai

The next references to Joshua in Exodus bookend several chapters (25-31) in which the Lord gave instructions to Moses with regard to the tabernacle while Aaron, Hur and the elders were left behind to take care of the people. Joshua, in his role as Moses' attendant, accompanied Moses at least part of the way up the mountain, if not to the top, where he appears to have remained while Moses received his instructions (Exodus 24:13).

The description in the text is awe-inspiring and frightening. For six days the cloud of the Lord's presence covered the mountain, and on day seven the Lord summoned Moses to enter the cloud. We're told that from the bottom of the mountain, 'the glory of the LORD looked like a consuming fire' (Exodus 24:17).

As we have already seen, the people became impatient and incited Aaron to produce a golden calf, which they worshipped (Exodus 32). Joshua was with Moses as he made his way down the mountain and he mistook the sounds of revelry in the camp for the sounds of war (v17). Of course, he was wrong, and it was the older, more experienced Moses who realised that the people in fact had run wild (v18). Perhaps we wonder which outcome, war or unrestrained and idolatrous revelry, would have been worse.

We can only try to imagine what kind of impression the subsequent scenes in the camp must have made on Joshua. What had got into these people who were running wild in an orgy of idolatry? What would he have made of Moses' command that the men were to take their swords and kill their friends? Or the fact that it happened (vv27-28)?

If the battle with Amalek was a vivid lesson in dependence, and forty days spent on the mountain must have left an impression of awe and holy mystery, what he saw in the camp must have marked him with a sense of the fickleness of the people and the challenge of pure devotion to the Lord.

Formative experiences

Leadership research has drawn attention to a range of terms that describe the ways in which leaders are shaped by their experiences: examples include 'tipping points', 'momentous events', 'defining moments' and 'crucibles'. In their book *Lessons of Experience*, Morgan McCall and his colleagues suggest that the development of a leader depends partly on raw talent, 'but also on the experiences one has and what one does with them'.[144]

While the Old Testament text does not go into detail about how Joshua may have processed his set of 'momentous events', it's clear that this young, emerging leader was being exposed to a range of remarkable experiences. For Joshua, leadership development was certainly not restricted to a ten-week course in a classroom, complete with a reflective essay or two, and signed off with a certificate to hang proudly on the wall of a study: food for thought for anyone involved in the training of young leaders.

At the tent of meeting

The picture is further developed when we read about the tent of meeting in Exodus 33. This tent appears to be

---

[144] Morgan W McCall, Michael M Lombardo, Ann M Morrison, *The Lessons of Experience: How Successful Executives Develop on the Job* (New York: The Free Press, 1988), p5.

different from the tabernacle that would later form the focal point of Israel's engagement with God. It was pitched some distance outside the camp and functioned as a place where Moses would meet with God and to which Israelites could go in order to enquire of the Lord.

Here, Moses lived out a remarkable relationship with God: 'The LORD would speak to Moses face to face, as one speaks to a friend' (Exodus 33:11). When Moses returned to the camp, Joshua stayed on – perhaps to prevent unauthorised entry into the tent.

Again we wonder what the impact of being in close proximity to Moses on these occasions must have been on Joshua. There is something special about being close to those who seem to have a distinctive relationship with God.

One of the people who influenced me when I was in my early twenties was Ralph Shallis. Ralph was an Englishman who had served God in North Africa before having to leave and settle in France. He went on to have a considerable influence on many in the French-speaking world. I had the opportunity to hear him speak when I was a student and later had the privilege of getting to know him personally. It may sound quite nerdy, but for my wife and me, part of what you might call our pre-courtship consisted of working together on the translation (from French) of one of his books![145] I once visited him and his wife in their home in southern France and sometime later

---

[145] Ralph wrote for the French-speaking Christian world, leaving it to others to translate his work if they wished. Only one of his books, *From Now On* (Port Colborne, ON: Gospel Folio Press, 2006), was published in English (not the one we worked on).

arranged for him to visit Northern Ireland to speak at a couple of gatherings.

Ralph walked closely with the Lord. As a young man he had decided to give God a daily tithe of his time: two and a half hours devoted to prayer and Bible reading. He recommended getting a new Bible every year, reading through it and marking various themes, using a colour code. It was best to start with a new Bible each year so that you would not simply regurgitate the previous year's thoughts. I have a Bible from my student days that is heavily marked by coloured pencils: I've read it and marked it following Ralph's method. The time he spent with the Lord told. With his white beard and somewhat mystical manner, he could have passed for Moses himself, emerging from the tent of meeting!

There was something almost other-worldly about him. I remember him on one occasion being so absorbed in praying for a meal in a restaurant that he didn't realise the waiter had arrived. A small, simple thing, perhaps, but he loved to talk to Jesus.

The thing about him – and others like him – is that there is something about their relationship with the Lord that seems to rub off on you when you talk with them. They breathe an atmosphere of prayer. It's as though they bring Jesus near.

I wonder what impact being close to Moses as the Lord spoke with him had on Joshua. How much of this – and so much more, as he watched Moses' reliance on the Lord and the way the Lord stepped in to provide and protect – stayed with him and coloured his hearing of the promise: 'As I was with Moses, so I will be with you' (Joshua 1:5)?

Eldad and Medad

In Chapter Four we reflected on a further incident where the Old Testament text brings Moses and Joshua together – the Eldad and Medad episode in Numbers 11. For some reason these two men, both listed as elders of the people (v26), had not gathered with the other elders when the Lord took some of the power of the Spirit that was on Moses and distributed it among them. The result of this impartation was that the elders prophesied. Although Eldad and Medad were not part of this gathering, having stayed on in the camp, the Spirit also rested on them and they prophesied where they were. A young man brought news of what was happening to Moses.

Joshua reacted with concern and asked Moses to stop the two prophets. Rather than stop them, Moses replied:

> Are you jealous for my sake? I wish that all the
> LORD's people were prophets and that the LORD
> would put his Spirit on them!
> (Numbers 11:29)

The text does not elaborate on the content of Eldad and Medad's prophecy, but instead draws attention to the theme of Joshua's jealousy. Was Joshua feeling threatened by the prophetic anointing of these two men? Or – as Moses himself suggested – was it more that he was jealous for his master? Dennis Cole suggests that 'Joshua perhaps sees these two men who were not directly under Moses' supervision as a threat to Moses' leadership'.[146] After all,

---

[146] Cole, *Numbers*, p195.

Joshua had been Moses' assistant since his youth (v28): Moses may have been the only significant leader he had ever really known.

Moses did not feel threatened either by the content of the prophecy or by the identity and motives of the prophets, but rather expressed his desire that all the Lord's people would prophesy and the Lord would put His Spirit on all of them.

Loyalty is a valued quality. No leader wants to turn around, like Shakespeare's Julius Caesar, and see his friend, Brutus, among the assassins! Yet loyalty can be distorted, and not only can a distorted form of loyalty blind a follower to the flaws of a leader, but it can also lead to a spirit of factionalism, where loyalty becomes narrow and blinkered and the wider picture is lost from sight.

One day John, Jesus' disciple, told his Master that the disciples had seen someone 'driving out demons' in His name. The problem was that this person was not one of them, not part of their group. So they tried to stop him (Luke 9:49).

At this point in their journey with Jesus, there was no doubting the loyalty of John and the other disciples. In fact, that loyalty will be underlined in the next incident that Luke recorded, where we find the disciples offering to 'call fire down' on a Samaritan village that had refused to welcome Jesus (Luke 9:54). How dare these Samaritans treat their Master with such disrespect?

But in both instances their loyalty had become skewed, and if John had expected Jesus to affirm him for his display of allegiance, he would be disappointed. Instead of saying something like, 'Well done, John! Thanks for protecting our little group – whatever would we do if others were using My name?', Jesus gave John an answer that he was not expecting: 'Do not stop him ... for whoever is not against you is for you' (Luke 9:50).

It's true that in another context Jesus calls for loyalty when He says that whoever is not with Him is against Him (Matthew 12:30). Is one statement contradicting the other? The difference is more subtle. In the first statement it's a question of whether or not someone is opposed to the disciples, whereas in the second, Jesus was addressing the question of how someone relates to Him.

There was a narrowness in the disciples' hearts, a fear that God might use someone who was not part of their group.

Don't we find the same thing in expressions of contemporary Christianity? While I think that, for many, denominational distinctions are perhaps not the same high walls that they were a couple of generations ago, there is still an element of mild tribalism in some of our thinking. Some of us still struggle to fully accept that God might genuinely be at work in groups that don't dot their i's or cross their t's in exactly the same way as us. In fact, they even leave some of them undotted or uncrossed altogether, a major issue if you think the prime purpose of the Church is to ensure proper punctuation! Similarly, some of the more free-running groups (you know, the ones with loud music and extensive tattoos) have a hard time thinking that the Holy Spirit's presence might actually grace a gathering of the i-dotters!

Please don't take this to mean that theological precision or a desire to be as biblical as possible in practice are to be abandoned, but perhaps some of us need to have a wider vision of God's work in the world. If God only worked through the means of your carefully defined group, how strong would the global Church be? How effectively would the gospel be spreading?

Factionalism was one of the issues that overshadowed the life of the Church in first-century Corinth. Too much significance was attributed to various leaders. For Paul (a hero to some of them), 'neither the one who plants nor the one who waters is anything' (1 Corinthians 3:7): God is the one who makes everything grow.

Whatever loyalty Joshua may have felt towards Moses, and however jealous he might have been for Moses' status among the people, Moses' lesson to him was that the more widely the Spirit of the Lord was at work among the Lord's people, the better.

We do well to accept that.

The majority is not always right

Perhaps one of the best-known of all the episodes in Joshua's life took place when he was sent to explore Canaan as one of twelve representatives of the people. Their brief was to evaluate the land: the strength of its cities and the suitability of its soil, and its people – strong and many, or few and weak. They were to report back and, if possible, bring back with them some samples of Canaan's produce.

The answer was that Canaan was wonderful: flowing with 'milk and honey' (Numbers 13:27), just as God had promised Moses all the way back at the time of his commissioning (Exodus 3:8). The problem was that the people were powerful and the cities were strong. The conclusion of the majority report was that the dangers outweighed the benefits: grasshoppers had no chance of overcoming giants. The inevitable result of this report was to plunge the people into despair and instigate talk of going back to Egypt.

No doubt Joshua (and Caleb) had seen the same things as everyone else, but their message was different. Initially it was Caleb who took the lead with his rallying call: 'We should go up and take possession of the land, for we can certainly do it' (Numbers 13:30). Joshua joined him as they pleaded with the people not to turn away from what God wanted to give them: 'If the LORD is pleased with us, he will lead us into that land, a land flowing with milk and honey, and will give it to us' (Numbers 14:8).

I must confess to a little surprise that Joshua is not specifically named in Hebrews 11. I imagine some folk would have had him there ahead of Samson or Jephthah, but there was no popular vote on who was in or out. The fall of Jericho is mentioned in verse 30, so at least there is an allusion to his leadership and his faith (and he is mentioned elsewhere in the book – see Hebrews 4:8). But it was Joshua's faith, his confidence that if the Lord were with him, obstacles need not stand in the way, that marked him out from most of his peers. Indeed, it's striking that in its telling of Old Testament history, Hebrews 11 skips straight from the Red Sea to Jericho: there is a missing generation. That was Joshua's generation, and he (and Caleb) stood out by a country mile.

Ready for leadership

All of this means that when we get to the point where Moses realised that he would not get to complete the task he started, the answer to his prayer for the future well-being of his people was right in front of him in the person of Joshua. There was no need for panic at the prospect of a leadership vacuum, or for a sudden, even ill-prepared recruitment drive. In giving Joshua to the people in place of Moses, the Lord would be establishing a leader who had first learned to serve reliably, a leader who had been witness to some remarkable phenomena, and someone who had learned that if the Lord is with him, everything changes.

To return to some of the questions that were posed earlier in the chapter, such as how leaders should go about preparing younger leaders and whether there are particular qualities to look for, the story of Moses and Joshua teaches us to look for, and invest in, emerging leaders who have a capacity to serve and a living faith in God and His ability to keep His promises. As I have already said, it's not clear whether Moses was intentionally mentoring Joshua for his future role, but when the time came for the handover, Joshua was ready.

His leadership assignment would be different from that of Moses. Derek Tidball makes this observation:

> However much he had learned from Moses, and however great his admiration for him, Joshua was not to be his clone. Neither Moses nor his memory would be honoured if Joshua simply repeated what he had done, or led in the way he

had led. He was a different person, chosen and equipped, just as Moses had been in his day, to lead in the light of what lay ahead.[147]

Nonetheless, the same Lord who had been with Moses would be with Joshua (Joshua 1:5), and while his assignment was different, there is evidence that some of what he had observed in Moses had rubbed off on him. It's striking that in the aftermath of Israel's painful defeat at Ai (Joshua 7), Joshua's prayer was for the reputation and honour of the Lord (vv:8-9), thus a clear echo of some of what we have already seen about Moses' heart for the honour of the Lord (Numbers 14:13-16).

Finishing well?

In the most obvious reading of his story, Moses did not finish well: as Arthur Boers notes, '[his] story ended in tragedy, not triumph'.[148] His petulant act of faithless disobedience meant that God removed him from his leadership role. He had played a successful part in the first phase of God's plan – rescue from Egypt – but would miss out on the completion of the plan – possession of Canaan.

But perhaps in another sense he did finish well, in as far as he demonstrated a concern for the future of the people and ensured a smooth handover to the next leader. We know that in his longing to get to enter Canaan he had pleaded with the Lord, but he had to stop his pleading (Deuteronomy 3:23-26): henceforth his task would be to

---

[147] Tidball, *Lead Like Joshua*, p5.
[148] Boers, *Servants and Fools*, p33.

commission and encourage Joshua, who would lead the people into the land. This Moses did:

> Be strong and courageous, for you must go with this people into the land that the LORD swore to their ancestors to give them … The LORD himself goes before you and will be with you; he will never leave you nor forsake you. Do not be afraid; do not be discouraged.
> (Deuteronomy 31:7-8)

Can I ask how you would respond if that became your assignment as a leader? Not to be out in front, leading the charge, but to step back and make the encouragement of the next generation your focus. It is not always easy to let go of our position, to allow others to emerge from our shadow, and to see them lead further and better than we ever have. In that at least, Moses finished well.

Just under two years before his death from a heart attack when he was fifty-eight, Mike Ovey, principal of Oak Hill College, preached at an ordination service in London. Here is part of what he said:

> We want you to be better than us, we want you to be more faithful than us – we want you, spiritually speaking, to tower above us so that the cross of the Lord Jesus Christ stands high in this land and that men and women may know the blessings of eternal life. That is our dream for

you, that is our prayer for you, not that you are
as we are, but that you are better.[149]

He would have had no idea that, like Moses, his own
leadership race had almost been run but, again like Moses,
he had a vision for the future. This was his heart for the
next generation of leaders.

When the time comes, wise leaders know how to hand
on the baton. Perhaps those who manage it with the most
grace are those who have most deeply understood that
their leadership has been a gift from God.

Questions for reflection

- What do you look for in assessing the potential of
  younger, emerging leaders?

- How much of your leadership is focused on helping
  to equip and empower the next generation of leaders?

- At the end of Chapter One, you had the opportunity
  to reflect on people who have influenced you in your
  faith and leadership. How can your leadership be an
  example to the next generation of leaders?

---

[149] The complete talk can be retrieved at
www.credomag.com/2017/01/mike-oveys-pastoral-wisdom-for-
future-ministers-of-the-gospel/ (accessed 22nd December 2020): the
extract cited begins at 26:07.

Epilogue
Wise Leaders Don't Get in the Way of Jesus

This is my Son, whom I have chosen; listen to him.
(Luke 9:35)

For leaders to *lead in the way* of Jesus is one thing (a good thing, if it means they are seeking to be like Him), but for leaders to *get in the way* of Jesus is something else.

Once more to Meribah

By way of a final word on Moses' leadership journey (and our own), we return once more to Meribah, and the rock-striking episode found in Numbers 20.

It was at Meribah that Moses' anger re-emerged. What had been an arguably reasonable attribute when he responded either to injustice or to the people's unfaithfulness was this time an expression of frustration as the complaints of the people tipped him over the edge. It led him to take a situation into his own hands, to deal with it in his own way, instead of trusting God and leaving room for Him to work, thus acknowledging His holiness.

Centuries later, referring to Israel's history by way of warning the members of the church in Corinth about the dangers of an array of sins, including putting Christ to the test, Paul wrote about the spiritual food and drink that were available to Moses' followers. They drank 'spiritual drink' from a 'spiritual rock', 'and that rock was Christ' (1 Corinthians 10:4).

I don't think Paul's reference requires a non-historical understanding of the incident at Meribah, but it does point us towards a typological understanding of the incident: in the desert, Christ was the true source of the people's nourishment.

The task of new covenant ministers is to share Christ with people. He is the source of spiritual life and nourishment that people need. Beyond what Paul says here in this somewhat enigmatic paragraph, Jesus referred to Himself as both 'the bread of life' (John 6:35) and the Source of 'living water' (John 4:10, 14). Our task is to help people to engage with Him.

May God forgive us when our words and actions get in the way of this and we drag His name into disrepute. How many people have been turned away from the Source of living water because of the behaviour or attitude of a Christian leader? It's a tragedy when people cannot see past us to Jesus. Our calling is to point to Him, to guard the sense of His holiness and to make sure that we do not make ourselves the focus.

May God forgive us when we do make ourselves the focus of our leadership. It's not simply the big-platform, high-profile leaders who are at risk (wittingly or not) of this. Any of us has the capacity at least to attempt to put ourselves at the centre. What good is our leadership if we get in the way of Jesus?

Those of us who are preachers need to be aware of the temptation to allow our frustrations to come out in the administration of harsh verbal lashes. There is something wearisome about the kind of preaching that seems to see listeners as a badly behaved class of children who need to be brought into line. Some good friends in our church in Switzerland were once kind enough to ask me if I liked Christmas (I do). They had noticed that in my zeal to 'challenge' the once-a-year visitors to our Christmas services, I was coming across as angry: Ebenezer Scrooge in the pulpit!

Recently I heard the story of advice that the Puritan Richard Sibbes gave to the seventeenth-century English preacher Thomas Goodwin. In Goodwin's own words, his preaching could be described as 'battering consciences'. After hearing him preach, Richard Sibbes said this: 'Young man, if you ever would do good, you must preach the gospel and the free grace of God in Christ Jesus.'[150]

There are times when, in our zeal, we simply try too hard. It's for the best of motives, but our ministry and leadership are all about 'challenge'. Our preaching is always about the big stick. Our leadership is always about the next hill to climb, rarely pausing long enough to be thankful for the distance we have already covered. Of

---

[150] Quoted by Michael Reeves:
www.uniontheology.org/resources/doctrine/jesus/foreword-to-richard-sibbes-josiahs-reformation (accessed 11th February 2021).

course, there is such a thing as a sense of urgency, but it's possible to try so hard that we end up getting in the way of Jesus. People grow weary, and it seems as though we are only offering stale bread and lukewarm water while all along Jesus wants to invite people to taste the 'bread of life' and to drink of the 'living water'.

'Listen to him'

The final piece of biblical narrative that involves Moses comes in the story of Jesus' transfiguration. Peter, James and John, the inner circle of His disciples, accompanied Him to pray on a mountain, where Moses and Elijah appeared and engaged in conversation with Jesus about what lay ahead in Jerusalem (Luke 9:31). After Peter's misguided suggestion about building a shelter each for Jesus and the two Old Testament figures, a cloud covered them and a voice spoke:

> This is my Son, whom I love; with him I am well
> pleased. Listen to him!
> (Matthew 17:5).

When their vision cleared, the only leader they could see was Jesus (v8).

And that is a good place for us to conclude. Our reflections have been framed in the story of a towering leader-figure, but one who was flawed. At the start of his leadership he attempted to wriggle out of God's call; later, he sabotaged his leadership through anger, and his story ended with disappointment.

The only flawless leader is Jesus, perfect in obedience, love and humility.

Listen to Him!

Wise leaders set themselves to walk in His ways, and they take care not to get in His way.